101
Great Mission
Statements

101
Great Mission Statements

HOW THE WORLD'S LEADING
COMPANIES RUN THEIR BUSINESSES

COMPILED BY TIMOTHY R V FOSTER

KOGAN
PAGE

This book is dedicated to my father, Leslie V Foster

First published in 1993, reprinted 1995

Kogan Page Limited
120 Pentonville Road
London N1 9JN

© Timothy R V Foster and contributors 1993

British Library Cataloguing in Publication Data

A CIP record for this book is available from the British Library.

ISBN 0–7494–0952–5

Typeset by BookEns Ltd., Royston, Herts.
Printed and bound in Great Britain by Clays Ltd, St Ives plc.

Contents

CONTENTS

CONTENTS

CONTENTS

Introduction

I have been fascinated by mission statements since I started getting involved in helping companies to put them together in the 1980s. I've been gathering them for several years, and this book represents the beginning of what I trust will be an interesting series of published collections. Yes, can *101 More Great Mission Statements* be far off?

All the statements included here are the most recent available, were supplied by the organisation in question and are used with permission. Appropriate copyrights are acknowledged.

Slogos

I have used my own service, Foster's Database of Slogos (see page 138), to come up with the most recent corporate or brand slogan or tag line for many of the organisations. These are printed *"in quotes and bold italics"* beneath the entity's name. Some outfits have several slogos, so I've just used one that is reasonably current. In any event, it's all part of their heritage.

Spelling

Usually one keeps to a house style in putting a book together, using one standard of spelling or another. Since the sources of the statements are so diverse, we have decided to leave the spelling as it is in the source document, so you'll see programme and program and organization and organisation, etc.

Acknowledgements

My thanks to Geoff Nightingale and Ferry de Bakker, two great friends and people who are at the cutting edge of mission statement technology, for their contributions. I also want to thank all the people in the corporate affairs and public relations departments of the organisations covered for their help and cooperation in getting the information I needed. And I definitely want to acknowledge my relationship with Burson-Marsteller, which has proved so valuable and exciting over the years. They really know how to help put the *mission* in the *statement*.

Chapter 1
Some Observations

It is my mission in this book to produce a valuable resource for people who want to know more about where organisations stand, what drives them, what makes them tick. To boldly go where no book has gone before – not at these prices, anyway!

According to Guy Kawasaki, author of *The Macintosh Way*, in his latest book, *Selling the Dream* (HarperCollins), 'A mission acts as a lantern, an anchor, and at times, a conscience. This is true whether you are a business or a non-profit organization.' Guy goes on to suggest that 'Good mission statements exhibit three qualities:

- *Short*. Brief and simple mission statements are easy to understand and remember. Brevity and simplicity are also evidence of clear thinking. For example, the Girl Scouts' mission statement is: "To help a girl reach her highest potential." It's short, simple, easy to understand, and easy to remember.

- *Flexible*. Flexible mission statements last a long time. For example, "ensuring an adequate supply of water" is inflexible and confining. It may not survive the next rainy season. The Macintosh [of Apple Computer] Division's mission statement was: "To improve the creativity and productivity of people." It was flexible enough to accommodate a computer and peripheral products such as laser printers, software, books and training for a long time.

- *Distinctive*. Distinctive mission statements differentiate your cause from other organisations with similar missions. The Centre for Living with Dying's mission statement, 'To provide emotional support for the dying and bereaved', sets it apart from most other non-profit and humanitarian organizations in Silicon Valley.'

(Excerpt © 1991 Guy Kawasaki, used with permission)

Some of the mission statements in this book follow these suggestions – a couple are less than one line of text in length. Others (my own included) tend to rabbit on a bit.

It's fascinating to read a lot of mission statements together. You get some interesting insights. The statements in this book are arranged alphabetically, and the category index groups them by line of business: airlines, computer makers, and so on.

Mission statements are not just for organisations. Dr John Viney is the UK chief of leading headhunters Heidrick & Struggles. He has written a book, with Dr Stephanie Jones, called *Career Turnaround – How to apply corporate strategy techniques to your own career* (HarperCollins/Thorsons). In it they suggest that individuals should create their own mission statements as part of their career-planning process.

They are kind enough to suggest some key words and phrases that might be helpful in creating a personal mission statement, and these are reprinted here, with permission.

Key words and phrases

Qualities
- strength
- soundness
- balance
- thrust
- creditworthiness
- solid foundations in changeable conditions
- innovation and efficiency
- management and financial resources to build on progress
- experienced yet still enthusiastic
- talented, with a speciality that's the key to future success

- hard-working, creative and cooperative
- professionalism with respect and appreciation for others
- able to manage risks and opportunities
- information conscious
- truly international

Experiences
- a history stretching back many years
- activities that spread far beyond national borders
- reputation for professionalism
- climbing many mountains, but always looking beyond to the next
- a confidence and inspiration that comes from the consistency of goals and philosophy
- innovation in many spheres of activity
- never a passive role
- an important contributor

Aims
- build business
- temper the pursuit of long-term aims with care and prudence
- plan, develop and continuously adapt to change
- aim to provide outstanding service
- be dedicated to excellence and success
- enhance the value of work for others
- steadfastly maintain values
- refocus resources on the areas of greatest potential return
- become leaner, more cost efficient, more competitive
- inaugurate imaginative policies and expand activities
- respond quickly to social changes.

All right! Taking the position that you have to be involved with a process in order to understand and accept it, and in order to be a true participant and not just a reporter, my own personal mission statement is on pages 138–9.

Corporate values study

In 1992, Digital Equipment Company sponsored a survey of executive opinion in the UK. It is called *Corporate Values, 'The Bottom Line Contribution'*, and was produced by its Management Counsel service under the guidance of leading consultant John Humble. They surveyed 429 managers of UK companies, covering a broad cross-section of industry and commerce, including industrial and consumer goods manufacturing, banking and financial services and distribution.

Defining corporate values as 'the relatively few important beliefs which are widely held to be crucial for the success of a given organisation; those beliefs and convictions which substantially drive the behaviour of people in an organisation', the survey found that:

- 80 per cent of organisations already have written value statements
- 89 per cent expect values to be more important for organisational success in the next three years
- 82 per cent believe that properly implemented values contribute to profitability

According to the survey, the top five priorities of these managers were:

- People – 'We believe our staff represent a crucial asset for our success'
- Competitiveness – 'We are committed to providing our customers with quality and service which beats the competition'
- Customers – 'We are totally dedicated to providing our customers with service that meets their needs'

- Quality – 'We are committed to delivering goods and services which meet the highest objective standards'
- Productivity – 'We must constantly increase the productivity of every resource in the organisation'

The two lowest priorities were:

- Social responsibility – 'In all our dealings we aim to behave with total integrity'
- Profitability – 'We believe that short-term profit is essential for our survival'

The survey went on to determine whether values influence practical decisions. The question raised was: 'Are your organisation's corporate values really slogans which do not make much difference to your daily work behaviour?'

- 6 per cent agreed
- 53 per cent said they 'partly made a difference'
- 39 per cent said that values really do make a difference

In answer to the question: 'If corporate values interfere with short-term commercial gain (especially in a recession), which gets priority?'

- 23 per cent said corporate values
- 30 per cent said commercial gain
- 38 per cent said both equally

The report suggests the following action steps to help management translate corporate values into bottom line benefits:

- 'Our corporate values – are we getting the bottom line benefits?' Place this item on your next board meeting agenda, with the aim of obtaining the commitment of directors to translate values into action
- Develop a vision for your company that embodies your corporate values

- Communicate that vision throughout your organisation and encourage managers to involve employees in action planning to make it happen
- Live the vision by taking decisions and actions that are consistent with your corporate values and make sure you are seen to be doing this
- Be seen to reward and recognise behaviour that is exemplary, in terms of corporate values
- Regularly review the extent to which values are translated into action and be prepared to challenge their relevance in the light of changes in your business environment

The above material was sourced from the report, sponsored and copyrighted by Digital Equipment Company, *Corporate Values: 'The Bottom Line Contribution'*. Copies of the report are available at no charge from Management Counsel, telephone (UK) 0256 371200 or by writing to Department 101, Management Counsel, PO Box 601, Reading RG1 7BR.

What does a mission statement say about the organisation?

Does a mission statement mean what it says? You'd hope so. But whose mission statement do you suppose this is?

'We aim, by excellence of management and pre-eminence in technology, to grasp the great opportunities created by the ever-increasing worldwide demand for information, prosperity and peace.'

That was the mission statement of Maxwell Communications plc, headed by the late fraudster, Robert Maxwell.

Of course you'd never expect to see something like this:

*'We aim, through the consistent and creative application of double dealing, contempt, bullying, lying, subterfuge, connivance, theft and fraud, to cheat our investors, our employees, our pensioners, our suppliers and other business partners and the regulatory bodies of the countries where we choose to operate, or **die** in the attempt!'*

Please do not judge us!

It is interesting to note that many of the companies contacted to provide their mission statements and agree to their use in this book insisted that we reproduce them without judgement of any kind. I pointed out that the title *101 Great Mission Statements* implied judgement of a sort, but since I have agreed to run their statements without judgement, I'll let you be the judge. What could they be afraid of?

A mission statement, what's that?

A few times, as I assembled this text, the question 'Do you have a mission statement?' was met with 'We certainly do! Would you like a copy?' And other times, it got the telephonic equivalent of a blank stare. Sometimes the device we print herein is not referred to by the organisation as a mission statement. Perhaps a corporate philosophy, a credo or a set of values is the term used. My measurement standard is 'could this be called a mission statement?'

Let's find out. But first, here's a little help from my friends.

Chapter 2
Successful Mission Management

By Geoffrey J Nightingale
President, SynerGenics Division
Young & Rubicam Inc, New York

The mission statement: is it a true, strategic management tool, or merely an overblown symbol of some company's or some chief executive's ego? The fact is, most organisations enter into the process of developing a formal mission statement with the clear belief that those efforts are going to challenge management and employees alike, establish an environment which fosters and nurtures positive change and, over time, produce an enterprise that is far more powerful and successful than that which exists today.

Yet, according to data generated over a period of nearly a decade working with companies in both Europe and North America, it is apparent that the majority (approximately 60 per cent) of mission statement programmes fail to achieve anywhere near the benefits initially anticipated. And having worked with some senior managers who have succeeded and with others who have failed in efforts to bring their mission statements to life, I have learned that it is the process, and not the product, that usually determines whether or not a mission statement becomes an effective management tool.

Experience indicates that the true value of a mission statement is always determined by the ability of management to use it effectively to focus the attention of the organisation on the task of anticipating and managing change. In that process:

- Management must act quickly and effectively to galvanise themselves and other levels of the organisation into a true team that is committed to and driven by a clear, shared, vision (mission) for success.

- They must enrol the entire organisation in that same

vision and empower their people and business partners to make the necessary changes to bring that vision to life.

- They must sweep aside any and all barriers to success by involving their people in activities that are uniquely focused on generating success through breakthrough results in operations, sales, service, technology, human resource development, administration, etc.

- They must take control of their positioning and image out in the marketplace and effectively manage important outside attitudes and opinions about the organisation, its management, and its product and service offerings.

And, in today's chaotic environment, management must do all of this at the same time as they are consolidating and restructuring, working themselves out of a recession, responding to the needs and demands of a rapidly changing marketplace and dealing with redundancies. No easy task!

The process begins with the creation of a formalised statement of mission. It does not end until the task of bringing the mission to life has been successfully completed. And at that point, the cycle begins anew.

The mission statement defined

We define a mission statement as follows:

> A statement of vision, or ambition that defines success and establishes the ground rules by which success will be achieved for a particular company or institution; the articulation of management's intent regarding the future of an organisation, expressed in aspirational terms.

The process we have found to be most effective in terms of its ability (a) to generate full consensus and commitment to a single mission by all members of management, and (b) to bring that mission to life throughout the organisation, consists of four steps leading up to a three-day, interactive, senior management workshop, during which time both the mission statement and the mission statement support programme are formulated.

It is critical that this process be directed and conducted by some disinterested third party – either an internal facilitator who has the trust and respect of top management, or an outside consultant with the experience and leadership skills to lead the project.

The process begins with:

- Individual interviews with the top two levels of management in the organisation to gauge commonalities and conflicts in attitudes, opinions and strategic thinking.
- A complete review of available documents, speeches, etc, in order to cross-check:
  — feelings about the present strategy and image of the company inside the organisation
  — the strategy and image that are being projected
  — how key managers envision the organisation furthering their vision
  — any barriers or gaps that they see as potentially getting in the way.
- At the same time, you will need some sort of an outside-in point of view on the company's strategy and image. That too is available through review of a variety of secondary sources – press clippings, analyst reports, etc. These data must be integrated with insights developed during the interviews.
- Using the work completed thus far, assemble a detailed summary on the findings, selected background reading material and a set of related exercises in the form of a briefing document. This document should be distributed to all members of the senior management team to give them time to prepare themselves adequately to contribute to the interactive workshop.

Final project design

The facilitator should design and conduct that workshop to ensure the senior management team is led through a series of consensus-building exercises leading to the writing of a clear, committed, statement of mission. To complete those exercises successfully, the participants must reach agreement on:

- A clear definition of the overall business
- The critical strengths and leverageable assets of the new organisation
- A picture of the future business environment looking forward four to five years
- Key success factors for the organisation in terms of that environment

Based on that work, the management team should then be taken through a series of focused creative sessions culminating in the creation of and commitment to the formal mission statement. All this should be accomplished during the first day of the workshop.

During the second day the management team should spend their time exploring areas of major synergy internally, and set up action plans for capturing those synergies in the shortest amount of time possible. They must also identify the critical barriers that could stop the organisation from achieving its vision and agree on the steps required and the responsibilities for dealing with those barriers. It is in this part of the process that the participants achieve 'ownership' for the various activities that they are recommending for implemention within the organisation.

On the third day of the workshop, the participants should reach consensus on a plan to build awareness, understanding and commitment to the new vision throughout the organisation, and agree on the initial steps for beginning work immediately.

Follow-up work should include the following activities:

- The fundamental process used in the off-site management meeting would be used in a series of meetings to develop unit strategies in support of the company vision and to build ownership for those ideas through the organisation.

- Subsequently, a company-wide action programme should be initiated, focused on bringing the new vision to life and aimed at creating an environment in which people are motivated to generate 'performance that matches the promise of the vision' – not simply on a one-time, campaign basis, but as part of their normal, day-to-day activities.

Action programme development

Base your programme on this ten-step model:

1 Identify the participating units (departments) and select a project leader from each unit to serve on the project committee
2 Set up the project committee and meet with them to:
   — Introduce them to the plan
   — Identify performance and project opportunities
   — Generate input for initial workshop
3 Meet with the project committee (two days) to:
   — Generate the projects and identify the measurements for the programme
   — Identify work teams and participants
   — Commit to the programme
   — Finalise programme design
4 Conduct participants' (work team) workshop
   — Align all participants on the new mission and commitments; achieve commitment to the programme and their participation in it
   — Train in project management, problem solving, communications, teamwork and creativity
   — Assign activities; set timetables
   — Finalise measurement and tracking system
5 Conduct coaching sessions with project teams
   — Ensure proper application of methodology and process in terms of actual projects
   — Facilitate handling of problems
6 Meet with project committee and other members of management throughout the programme

   — Continually oversee and monitor progress relative to
      goals
7 Two-month review and training
   — Two-day participants' workshop
   — Focus on deepening and reinforcing the commitment
      and process
   — Address any problems, issues that have surfaced
   — Give participants a chance to share experiences
   — Monitor and measure
8 Follow-up coaching sessions
   — Continue driving results; on-the-spot training
9 Four-month review and training
   — Same as item 7 above
10 Final project committee meeting
   — Results reported and assessed
   — Plan for spreading programme developed and agreed
      upon

Where mission statement programmes fail

Based on the experience gained working with over 50
companies in the development and implementation of mission statement programmes, we have been able to identify
certain patterns of behaviour and activity which, left
unchecked, almost always result in programme failure. For
example:

- Lack of definition in the vision
  — Failure to build full understanding effectively, or to
    manage organisational interpretations of the mission
- Lack of management commitment
  — Cynicism, scepticism, uncertainty, resistance impacting
    all levels of the organisation
- Failure to actively enrol employees, the marketplace and
  other influentials in support of the mission
  — Ineffective communications based on all the above
- Lack of planning and focused implementation
  — Seeing the work of bringing the mission to life as a

'task', or added burden, rather than as fundamental to the job

- Inability to deal effectively with breakdowns as they occur, representing a lack of commitment, or a lack of skill

In the final analysis, a mission statement can be a uniquely powerful management tool. And you can put that potential to work for you, but only if you commit to five fundamental rules in the creation and implementation of your mission statement programme:

- Be absolutely authentic and honest in your preparations
- Select a process that works and stick with it
- Avoid getting seduced and trapped into engaging in potentially harmful short cuts
- Take the time and make the effort to build your mission statement support activities into the day-to-day business practices of your organisation – from top to bottom
- Anticipate problems and deal with them before they occur by creating effective contingency plans

Above all, remember this: the one factor which is always present in a successful mission statement programme is the active leadership and support of senior management on a continuing basis.

Chapter 3
The Elements of a Mission Statement

By Ferdinand de Bakker
General Manager, Burson-Marsteller/The Hague

Mission statements usually have five key components. They are:

- A description of the business the organisation is in
- The mission of the organisation, sometimes broadly stated, sometimes described as a short and powerful strategic intent
- The organisation's assets, or key strengths
- Broad strategies to be pursued in order to achieve the mission
- The values the organisation adheres to in pursuit of its mission

Description of the business

This should include a description of the organisation's customers, its products and services, and the geographical locations in which it does business, although it is also possible to refer to these components when describing the core mission.

Describing the core mission may seem simple, but once brought together, senior managers of organisations practically always have a problem defining it.

When, for example, top management of a major European bank got together recently to discuss this, the inevitable first answer to that simple question was 'a bank'. Then it became 'a financial institution', but as it turned out this bank also had a travel agency, was involved in insurance, participated in a joint-venture in telecommunications and had stakes in real estate developments.

One of the leading global direct marketing firms didn't even want to use its key discipline, direct marketing, to describe its business, but went for advertising agency instead, only to be corrected by its middle management when the top executives presented the statement. And if that hadn't happened, the marketplace would, no doubt, have rejected it.

Should the 'statement of the business we're in' be looked at from the organisation's perspective, or from the customer's viewpoint? If we use the latter, you would get something like: 'We're in the business of satisfying customer needs in the area of personal and business finance.' However, if a bank representative gives this answer when asked what his employer is doing, he stands a pretty good chance of not being understood. So, in general, it is better to describe it from the organisation's own perspective.

Also, executives have a tendency to make this an all-encompassing description which nobody, apart from those who produced it, will understand. The chairman of the board of directors of a major European construction conglomerate told me that he and his colleagues sat in total astonishment and ended up completely confused when the board of management presented a statement which, roughly, sounded like:

'We're in the business of initiating, suggesting, designing, engineering, developing, creating, servicing and managing public and private projects such as private and public housing, utilities, office buildings, shopping complexes, harbours, pipelines, roads and other infrastructural works on our own or in joint-ventures for individuals, private industry, building associations, harbour authorities, city, regional and national authorities and any other parties through our divisions and business units, including dredging and reclamation, civil engineering and construction, pipelines, roads and housing operating in 12 countries in Europe and elsewhere in the world where we decide to do business.'

Otis Elevator Company, part of United Technologies, managed to produce a much shorter yet very accurate statement in one of its internal strategic plans – and one which is easy to remember: 'Moving people and material vertically and horizontally over relatively short distances.' And the Kowloon Canton Railway Corporation: 'To provide quality transport and related services in Hong Kong and within China in a safe, reliable, caring, cost effective and environmentally responsible manner.'

The mission

The mission, at its best a short description of the strategic intent, is the second and core element of a mission statement. Here, the organisation lays out and declares its ultimate and long-term goals, without getting into details. Sometimes, these statements of intent are specific, such as 'To become the world's number two manufacturer of commercial aircraft' (Airbus, early 1980s); 'To be the undisputed European leader, and to establish a strong position in the USA in training and consulting activities in management and sales' (Krauthammer International); 'To become the worldwide standard for international factoring' (Factors Chain International); and 'To become the acknowledged global leader in the express delivery of documents and packages' (DHL Worldwide Express).

Sometimes they are less specific, as the following example of Matsushita, dating back to May 1932, illustrates: 'The real mission of Matsushita is to produce an inexhaustible supply of goods, thus creating peace and prosperity throughout the land.' Another not very specific example is that of Florida Power & Light: 'During the next decade, we want to become the best-managed electric utility in the United States and an excellent company overall and be recognized as such.' And Lufthansa's corporate philosophy states: 'Our aim is to provide the best possible quality. Our performance and efficiency are based on a modern fleet and dedicated personnel. These alone safeguard our future.'

This core mission must be attractive enough for people to buy into, yet far-reaching enough to drive the company for a longer period of time: Burson-Marsteller, the international public relations firm, describes it as 'a journey without end, but one with a distinct destination'. British Telecom says: 'To become the most successful worldwide telecommunications group.'

Key strengths

Some organisations are very specific in listing these although it always remains to be seen if they really are key strengths, particularly since unique strengths often are implicit weaknesses. NutraSweet's aspartame was, for many years, the organisation's key strength and at the same time it represented the company's most dangerous vulnerability, as NutraSweet, for many years, was a one-product company.

Some of these strengths are better defined as invisible assets and can play a major role as visible corporate resources: corporate culture, brand image, consumer trust, distribution and management skill: 'We will combine entrepreneurial zeal with prudent management to assure continued stability' (Akzo). They may be more powerful than some of the traditional visible assets, such as workers, inventory and capital, although these remain important to many entities: 'our people and their determination form the cornerstone of our success' (Philips Dictation Systems). A powerful combination was made by AMRO Bank, before it merged with ABN to become one of Europe's most powerful financial institutions: 'The company's strengths are to be found in its seamless domestic distribution network, its top quality corporate and private client base, its leadership position in investment banking and treasury, its superior technological infrastructure and in the dedication and quality of its employees and management.'

Strategy

Core strategies are no real secret and are a logical reflection of the company's positioning in the marketplace. They're part of the mission statement because the company's audiences, its stakeholders (people who have a stake in the company, such as employees, customers, investors, suppliers, etc), must have an awareness of how the organisation's management will 'get there'. These strategies are sometimes very defined, such as those laid out by Bank of America, which span four pages and are divided into:

- Corporate
  — business scope
  — customer focus
  — service emphasis
  — competitive approach
  — financial strategy
  — resource allocation
- Retail
  — California
  — National expansion

Ciba, the Swiss chemical and health-care corporation, divides its strategies into three areas: the products area, the marketplace and the organisation itself. Other organisations use different words to describe their strategies: 'basic concepts' (Andersen Consulting); 'priorities' (Beatrice; Johnson & Johnson); or even more direct and urgent: 'our costs must come down' and 'we must invest heavily in modern equipment and networks' (British Telecom).

Values

These represent the fifth and final element of mission statements. 'Matsushita believes in peace, brotherhood and market share.' Although this is a tongue-in-cheek statement, reflecting how outsiders perceive the organisation's values, it does indicate one of the difficulties in listing values.

Usually, management will agree on a set of values they believe are necessary for success, but often they don't represent the values the organisation currently adheres to. And listing values which just sound nice is dangerous, because for many employees they are the most important part of the mission statement. This is because management states what it expects, and what it is willing to give. And, as one might expect, most of these value statements are lopsided: the organisation expects everything and doesn't think about giving anything.

Dow Chemical's statement of core values, on the other hand, states that 'employees are the source of Dow's success. We treat them with respect, promote teamwork, and encourage personal freedom and growth. Excellence in performance is sought and rewarded.'

Some organisations have interesting sets of values. One management consultancy, for example, talks about the obligation to dissent, which encourages, or even forces, its consultants to question everything, inside the firm and outside.

Matsushita developed, in 1933, seven principles which remain today, as they have been since that time, the watchwords for the daily work of its tens of thousands of employees. They are:

- Spirit of service through industry
- Spirit of fairness
- Spirit of harmony and cooperation
- Spirit of striving for progress
- Spirit of courtesy and humility
- Spirit of accord with natural law
- Spirit of gratitude

The problem with some value statements is that employees read them and then look around. And it is here where most mission statement programmes are being killed. This is because management is judged constantly and its behaviour is benchmarked all the time against the values. Often there's no visible change in the behaviour of top management and so employees are encouraged to do the same. When John Burke, at that time CEO of Johnson & Johnson (which has produced one of the finest mission statements of all times), was faced with a product tampering case, back in 1981, he referred to J&J's Credo, as it's called, when he had to take sometimes very difficult and far-reaching decisions: 'We believe our first responsibility is to the doctors, nurses and patients, to mothers and fathers and all others who use our products and services.'

As you will notice, although many mission statements look alike, they're all unique – because they do reflect the vision and the thinking of top management. Some are more intent oriented, others are more values oriented. Lifetime employment, which may have been an element, or a value, in mission statements of organisations which truly believed in that concept will never appear again, because of the change in times. And so one can notice a shift in values, depending on the state of the global economy.

Finally, a word of caution: 'Grand, abstract visions can be too inspirational. The company may wind up making more poetry than product', writes Gerhard H Langeler, president of the Systems Group of Mentor Graphics Corporation, in a revealing article in the March/April 1992 issue of *Harvard Business Review*. The title of the article, 'The Vision Trap', warns readers to be very careful when developing mission statements because they may become too grandiose and beyond anyone's power, and as a consequence may not be 'bought' by the organisation's employees. Then they're bound to fail. And that's not quite what you're aiming for when you craft your mission statement.

Chapter 4
The Mission Statements

1 Aegis Group plc UK   Media specialists

Aegis is the holding company for Europe's largest group of media specialists which trade under the name Carat.

The Group's operating companies serve clients through media strategy, research, media planning and buying.

Aegis companies are market leaders and combine the power of volume buying with media expertise based on an unmatched investment in research and analysis of the media marketplace to provide clients with cost-effective access to target audiences.

Aegis is dedicated to creating wealth for its shareholders by recruiting and training the best people, and by continuing to win market share through superior client service.

Aegis has invested, and will continue to invest, in keeping its operating companies in a position of leadership to serve clients in the constantly changing and growing media market-place.

---

2 AMEC Group plc UK   Engineering

Group strategy
The AMEC Group has a comprehensive engineering, construction and development capability.

Our breadth and depth of resource give us the strength and flexibility to:

- Respond effectively to changing client requirements
- Adapt our services to meet every need
- Resist cyclical change
- Innovate and create opportunity

We aim to enhance the breadth of our integrated capability throughout the world.

We will continue to offer the highest quality of service, products and management, basing our growth on a sound foundation of financial prudence.

The main principles of our strategy are to:

- Offer our clients the broadest possible range of engineering, construction and development services
- Ensure that every service offered is the best in its market
- Offer our services wherever our clients need them, worldwide.

---

3 American Express USA   Travel related services

"Don't leave home without it"

Blue box values

All our activities and decisions must be based on, and guided by, these values:

- Placing the interests of **clients** and **customers** first
- A continuous **quest for quality** in everything we do
- Treating our **people** with respect and dignity
- Conduct that reflects the highest standards of **integrity**
- **Teamwork** – from the smallest unit to the enterprise as a whole
- Being **good citizens** in the communities in which we live and work

To the extent we act according to these values, we believe we will provide outstanding service to our clients and customers, earn a leadership position in our businesses and provide a superior return to our shareholders.

---

4 Andersen Consulting — Management consultants

"Metamorphosis in a world of change"

To help our clients change to be more successful.

---

5 Apple Computer USA — Computers

"The power to succeed"

Our mission statement
It is Apple's mission to help people transform the way they work, learn and communicate by providing exceptional personal computing products and innovative customer services.

- We will pioneer new directions and approaches, finding innovative ways to use computing technology to extend the bounds of human potential.
- Apple will make a difference: our products, services and insights will help people around the world shape the ways business and education will be done in the 21st century.

---

6 Automobile Assocation UK — Association

"We're all you need to know"

AA group mission
Our vision
To make AA membership truly irresistible

Our mission
To be the UK's leading and most successful motoring and personal assistance organisation

Our values
Courtesy and care for all our members and customers
Our people, and their skills
Our image of integrity and independence
Quality and value for money in all our services and products
Our business partners

---

7   BAA plc   Airports
   UK

"The world's leading international airport group"

Our mission is to make BAA the most successful airport company in the world.
We will:

- always focus on our customers' needs and safety
- seek continuous improvements in the costs and quality of our services
- enable our employees to give of their best

To achieve our mission we will:

Safety and security
Give safety and security the highest priority at all times

Strategy
Concentrate on the core airport business, be prudently financed, continuously improve quality and cost effective-

ness, fully develop our property and retail potential and achieve world class standards in capital investment

Customers
Ensure our customers receive excellence and good value in the services BAA provides

Employees
Provide a good and safe working environment which attracts and retains committed employees. Through training and two-way communication allow them to fulfil their potential and contribute directly to the success of the company

Shareholders
Encourage shareholders to believe in our company by giving them consistent growth in earnings and dividends

Environment
Recognise the needs of the local communities and be seen as a good neighbour with concern for the environment

---

8   Bass plc   Brewer
UK

"Bass, since 1876"

Statement of purpose
The Bass Group has grown from a base as a major brewer to encompass significant complementary businesses in branded drinks and hospitality retailing. It intends to be the preferred choice for customers in each of its markets by offering superior quality, service and value.

The Group's aim is to obtain attractive and increasing returns for shareholders.

Bass is committed to:

• Establishing a flexible, responsive and innovative corporate culture capable of leading change in the dynamic markets in which it competes

- Involving and developing the people working in its businesses, ensuring that they have the skills and motivation to outperform the competition
- Establishing the most competitive cost base for each business
- Investing in a first-class range of brands
- Investing in the underlying property assets of the business
- While mainly operating in the United Kingdom, Bass seeks to expand its products and services in wider geographical markets which offer potential for profitable growth

---

9   Bayer AG   Chemicals
Germany

Bayer is an international, broadly diversified chemical and health care company with operations in some 150 countries.

Its 23 Business Groups are organized within six sectors: Polymers, Organic Products, Industrial Products, Health Care, Agrochemicals and Imaging Technologies.

Our expertise lies in research, service, technology, quality and efficiency in all our areas of activity. This forms the basis for our success and safeguards the future.

We consider it our duty to use this expertise to benefit mankind, and to play our part in solving the major problems of our time.

Moreover, it is our responsibility to ensure the safety of our operations and to minimize their impact on the environment, while efficiently utilizing natural resources.

Bayer: Expertise with Responsibility

---

10   BBA Group plc   Industrials
UK

Mission statement: BBA – a corporate philosophy
The inertia of history is a powerful influence on corporate philosophy. BBA in its 103 years of existence has strayed little from:

(i)   Yorkshire paternalism.
(ii) Weaving of heavy textiles.
(iii) Friction technology via woven or pressed resin media.

The philosophy of BBA for the next few years will be to adapt rather than abandon the inert.

Management
(a) Grit and gumption are preferable to inertia and intellect.
(b) The Victorian work ethic is not an antique.
(c) One man can only serve one master, to whom he is responsible for a minimum number of succinctly defined tasks.
(d) Most companies owned or yet to be acquired possess adequate people waiting to be transformed by dedicated leadership.
(e) The effectiveness of an organisation is in inverse proportion to the number of hierarchical layers.

Markets
We shall concentrate on markets where:

(a) The products are in a state of maturity or decline 'sunset industries'.
(b) The scale of our presence in a market segment will allow price leadership.
(c) The capital cost of market entry is high.
(d) Fragmentation of ownership on the supply side facilitates rapid earnings growth by acquisition of contribution flows.

Money
(a) The longer run belongs to Oscar Wilde, who is dead.
(b) The key macro and micro variables of our business are so dynamic that poker becomes more predictable than planning and reactivity more profitable than rumination.
(c) Budgets are personal commitments made by management to their superiors, subordinates, shareholders and their self-respect.
(d) The cheapest producer will win.
(e) The investment of money on average return of less than three points above market should be restricted to Ascot.
(f) Gearing should not exceed 40 per cent. The location from which funds emanate should be matched to the location from which profit stream permits their service.
(g) We are not currency speculators, even when we win.
(h) Tax is a direct cost to the business and, accordingly, should be eschewed.
(i) Victorian thrift is not an antique.
(j) Nothing comes free, cheap assets are often expensive utilities.

Monday
Our tactic is to:

(i) Increase the metabolic rate of BBA through directed endeavour.
(ii) Increase profit margins by drastic cost reduction.
(iii) Massage and thereby extend the life cycle of the products in which we are engaged.
(iv) Become market dominant in our market niches by:
    (a) outproducing the competition;
    (b) transforming general markets where we are nobody to market niches where we are somebody;
    (c) buying competitors.
(v) Use less money in total and keep more money away from the tax man and the usurer.
(vi) Avoid the belief that dealing is preferable to working.
(vii) Go home tired.

Maybe
(a) The replication of our day-to-day tactic provides long-term growth.
(b) We need to address 'Monday' this week and what our reaction will be to what may be on 'Monday' for the next three years.
(c) Three years is, in the current environment, the limit of man's comprehension of what may be.
(d) Long-term growth necessitates:
  (i) Resource – notably men and money.
  (ii) Sustained performance rather than superficial genius.

---

11   The Boots Company plc   Drug retailing UK

"Who cares?"

Our objective is to maximise the value of the company for the benefit of its shareholders.
  We will do so:

• By building on our position as one of the UK's leading retailers in our chosen markets

• By investing in the research, development, manufacturing and marketing of innovative prescription pharmaceuticals and consumer healthcare products throughout the world

• Through enterprising development and management of our property assets

While vigorously pursuing our commercial interests we will, at all times, seek to enhance our reputation as a well managed, ethical and socially responsible company.

---

12 Bowater plc   Paper and packaging
UK

Bowater is first and foremost a Print and Packaging Group. Its skill is advanced design and manufacture of specialist elements for products which call on many technologies.

The Group also contains businesses in Industrial Films, Tissue, Building and Engineering, each of which makes a particular technical, market or geographic contribution to the whole. Yet they are not so tightly focused on their individual tasks that they cannot benefit from Bowater's parenting.

The Bowater of today is made up of a large number of businesses around the world, linked by technologies or markets. These linkages are expanding fast and help customers gain optimum benefit through partnering relationships with Group companies.

The underlying idea is that Bowater knows when to be small and when to be big.

Responsibility has been passed down the line in a democratic way. People dealing with Bowater encounter small-company commitment.

Bowater is small, therefore, in working through vigorous companies attacking niche markets. But it is big in being able to share expertise, monitor performance and invest.

Bowater invests to support its manufacturing policy of high reliability. It likes to operate in market areas where few competitors can measure up to demands.

Expertise is shared by networking within the Group. Even Bowater's internal address book indicates which companies have particular skills. Bowater has strong financial disciplines. Management information arrives in days not months and decisions on investment submissions in hours not weeks.

All this adds up to an open company. One which can exploit its abilities to grow profitably in selected sectors. The Group aims for management which is not tight but taut, for a Bowater which is not rigid and risk averse but well motivated to be permanently stretched.

13   British Airways plc   Airline
UK

"The world's favourite airline"

Our mission
To be the best and most successful company in the airline industry.

Our goals
Safe and secure
To be a safe and secure airline.

Financially strong
To deliver a strong and consistent financial performance.

Global leader
To secure' a leading share of air travel business worldwide with a significant presence in all major geographical markets.

Service and value
To provide overall superior service and good value for money in every market segment in which we compete.

Customer driven
To excel in anticipating and quickly responding to customer needs and competitor activity.

Good employer
To sustain a working environment that attracts, retains and develops committed employees who share in the success of the company.

Good neighbour
To be a good neighbour, concerned for the community and the environment.

---

14 British Gas plc UK   Gas

"A world class energy company"

Statement of purpose
We aim to be . . .
a world class energy company and the leading international
gas business by:

- Running a professional gas business providing safe, secure and reliable supplies
- Actively developing an international business in exploration and production of oil and gas
- Making strategic investments in other energy-related projects and businesses world wide
- Satisfying our customers' wishes for excellent quality of service and outstanding value
- Constantly and energetically seeking to improve quality and productivity in all we do
- Caring for the environment
- Maintaining a high quality workforce with equal opportunities for all
- Cultivating good relations with customers, employees, suppliers, shareholders and the communities we serve

and thereby improving returns to shareholders.

---

15 The British Library UK   Library

"The world's leading resource for scholarship, research and innovation"

Statement of purpose
The British Library, through its incomparable collections, is
the world's leading national research library. We have

expert staff and we give ready access to our collections in our reading rooms and by remote supply.

Our function is to serve scholarship, research and enterprise. Our purpose is to promote the advance of knowledge through the communication of information and ideas.

We celebrate and interpret our rich and varied collections to encourage the broadest possible awareness and accessibility of the nation's recorded heritage.

To achieve this:

- we identify and respond to our users' needs for a national library service;
- we build, catalogue and conserve the collections;
- we provide entry to the world's knowledge base;
- we provide leadership and initiate cooperative programmes for the national and international research library community; and
- we exploit our collections in enterprising ways to raise support for our activities.

We are committed to maintaining our position of leadership by embracing innovative, cost-effective and flexible methods of working.

---

16   British Midland UK   Airline

"The serious alternative"

The mission statement
British Midland is a major airline in the domestic scheduled service field, together with selected European operations.

Our mission is to improve our service to meet the customer's needs, allowing us to expand our business throughout Europe and in doing so, generate the necessary profit to develop our company.

---

17   British Nuclear Fuels plc   Energy
UK

To grow profitably, providing the world with the best nuclear services, safely, efficiently and with care for the environment.

---

18   British Telecom   Telecommunications
UK

"It's you we answer to"

Purpose
In a world of turbulent change, our aim in BT remains constant. It is summed up in our vision: *'To become the most successful worldwide telecommunications group.'*

Our purpose is described more fully in our mission: *'To provide world-class telecommunications and information products and services. To develop and exploit our networks, at home and overseas, so that we can:*

- *Meet the requirements of our customers*
- *Sustain growth in the earnings of the group on behalf of our shareholders*
- *Make a fitting contribution to the community in which we conduct our business'*

To achieve our vision, our costs must come down.

We are operating in a difficult business environment, where recession, competition and regulation are commercial facts of life.

To survive and prosper in this climate, we must invest heavily in modern equipment and networks and apply our skills to make the best use of the huge investment we have already made. Put more simply, today's technology means we must provide a better service with fewer people. If we don't somebody else will.

Quality imperatives
We must:

Drive quality from the top
Pursue excellence in customer service
Support BT people in achieving Total Quality
Set and achieve world-best standards of management

Customers
Now, more than ever before, there is a need for greater customer responsiveness – and we must do even more.

Customer commitment
We are committed to providing our customers with a helpful, polite and world-class service.
    We aim to give:

- *Value for money*
- *Excellent performance backed by guarantee*
- *Compensation if we fall short*
- *Continuously improving levels of service*
- *An easy way to deal with us, by phone or face-to-face*
- *Choice and control over how our services are used*
- *Options on prices and payment*
- *Attention to special needs*

By the end of 1993, we shall aim to provide service on demand – within one day, seven days a week – and to clear all faults within one day as well, or pay compensation.

People
Our success continues to depend on our people. That success hinges on our awareness of competition, of regulation and of our customers' perception of the value for money we offer. Our performance must match our promises – first time, every time – and we must build quality into everything we do.

19 BUPA   Health care provider
UK

"Purely for the benefit of your health"

BUPA vision statement
We will be pre-eminent in independent health care, delivering best value, highest quality, personal service to our customers in a caring manner.
    To do this we aim to:

1. Continue the traditions of providing help sensitively in times of need
2. Secure our future by operating profitably
3. Offer the best health care anyone can buy for the price they can afford
4. Earn and deserve the confidence of our customers, the community, the medical profession and government, by establishing BUPA as an outstandingly effective partner and contributor to the health care systems in which we work
5. Ensure that all internal and external communications are clear, honest and unambiguous
6. Ensure that all our employees are proud to be part of BUPA
7. Develop continuously the capabilities of each employee
8. Create new products and services that are valued by our customers
9. Improve constantly everything we do

---

20 Burson-Marsteller   Public relations
USA

"Imagination with substance, execution with style"

Our vision . . .
Burson-Marsteller has embarked on an adventure in communications . . . A journey without end; but one with a distinct destination.

We seek to build the most exciting counseling and communications organization in the world, adding new dimensions to the meaning of public relations and public affairs. The process is never ending; as the world changes, we will change with it. The only constant is our dedication to excellence in thought and deed.

The premises that drive us are simple but challenging. The consulting and communications organization that will rise above all others will be the one most relevant to the broadest range of client needs. It will be knowledgeable, strategically sound, but never timid . . . Efficient, executionally thorough, but never dull . . . Always reaching out to cross new frontiers.

We exist solely to serve our clients. Our client focus demands that we remain flexible, organic and dynamic so that we can apply our best resources to each client problem, program and project.

Ultimately, to be successful, we must be valued by our clients as true business partners, providing superior counsel and services that not only meet but anticipate their needs. We will not, however, allow client satisfaction to lead to complacency.

We recognize that there are no absolutes in our world . . . That we have no monopoly on people or product. We remain restless with what is, searching always for what could be. We will constantly seek out the best talent, the freshest ideas, the broadest concepts, the newest perspectives in our efforts to enhance our value to our clients.

Ours is a global business. It demands that we work to a single standard of excellence worldwide. We will build the systems and harness the technology that will give all our people, anywhere in the world, equal access to our knowledge, experience and skills.

Quality, innovation and value . . . Sensitivity to our clients and to each other . . . High energy, high reward . . . Impatience with the status quo . . . A willingness to take risks . . . Compulsive curiosity . . . These are our guideposts. And, while our destination will always be before us, it is absolutely essential we make the journey.

Our values . . .
We believe the most significant factor contributing to our company's progress has been an instinctive adherence to a unique set of values – rarely articulated, but always understood by our most successful people. Ours is a demanding business. High energy, hard work, even a high threshold of pain are constants at Burson-Marsteller. Given the pressures of our extraordinary growth, there is little room for any other kind of behavior. Beyond this, though, we admire certain qualities:

Achievement
The common thread that propels our most successful people is the constant need to excel, to achieve personal and professional goals beyond the expected norm. Our people are known for their results orientation. They are tireless in striving for real impact on their client's businesses, for demonstrable value. They seek to define the real problem, develop the real solution, no matter what the obstacles or the personal sacrifices required.

Teamwork
Ours is a multi-disciplinary business. Sound strategy and creative execution require diverse talents to work in unison. B-M people realize that individual success depends on cooperation and support. We prize the individual, but celebrate the team.

Commitment
We are profoundly committed to the goal. Our people let no obstacles interfere with the fulfillment of their responsibilities. We hold true to our word. Clients and colleagues alike can count on us.

Curiosity
B-M people are inherently uncomfortable with the traditional. They recognize that there is no such thing as a single, correct perspective on any issue or problem . . . that today's absolute truth is often tomorrow's folklore. They welcome

new knowledge, new insights, new ideas, no matter the source. At Burson-Marsteller, ideas have no rank, no country of origin. While the company endeavors to train and grow its people, we firmly believe the ultimate responsibility for personal growth is up to the individual.

Sharing
B-M people are quick to share information, knowledge and experience. All of us, at any given moment, are students, teachers or mentors. Our instinct is to accept all who wish to contribute; to reject those who would try to use knowledge as power. We hold mutual respect for our clients, peers, subordinates and superiors. We accept blame individually. We share credit collectively.

Risk
We encourage prudent risk. We reject the notion that if it hasn't been done, it won't work. If we think it's right, we want to do it. And we will fight for the opportunity.

---

21 Cadbury Schweppes plc   Foods
UK

Cadbury Schweppes is a major global company in beverages and confectionery whose quality brands and products are enjoyed in over 170 countries around the world.

Our task is to build upon our tradition of quality and value to provide brands, products, financial results and management performance that meet the interest of our shareholders, consumers, employees, customers, suppliers and the communities in which we operate.

---

22   Card Protection Plan Ltd   Credit
UK   card insurance

CPP's vision
To ensure that cardholders throughout the UK and Europe
are aware of the problems caused by card loss and to inform
them of the necessity of card protection, making it as widespread as home contents insurance in years to come.

CPP's mission
Judged as equal best provider of card protection in the
world by the industry's independent publication, *The Nilson
Report*, CPP's mission is to build on this reputation of providing an excellent service which continues to meet the
needs of its customers by:

- employing the most innovative and effective marketing
  techniques
- generating the highest response rates
- delivering the best quality service in every respect to
  policyholders and all card issuers
- maintaining the highest policy renewal rates in the industry

By achieving the above CPP ensures that, in comparison to
other providers, the greatest amount of commission income is
generated for its business partners.

---

23   The Coca-Cola Company   Soft drinks
USA

"Coke is it!"

Our opportunity
Bringing refreshment to a thirsty world is a unique opportunity for our Company . . . and for all of our Coca-Cola
associates . . . to create shareholder value. Ours is the only
production and distribution business system capable of realiz-

ing that opportunity on a global scale. And we are committed to realizing it.

Our goal
With Coca-Cola as the centerpiece, ours is a worldwide system of superior brands and services through which we, our franchisees and other business partners deliver satisfaction and value to customers and consumers. By doing so, we enhance brand equity on a global basis. As a result, we increase shareholder wealth over time.

Our goal for the 1990s sounds deceptively simple. It is to expand our global business system, reaching increasing numbers of consumers who will enjoy our brands and products more and more often.

Our challenge
The 1990s promise to be a paradoxical time for our business. Distribution channels will continue to consolidate while new ones will emerge . . . yet, customers will demand more choices, as well as customized service and marketing programs at the lowest possible cost. Consumers in developed countries will grow in age and affluence but not in numbers . . . while strong population growth in lesser developed countries means the vitality of these young consumer markets will depend on job creation and expanding economies.

To succeed in this environment we will make effective use of our fundamental resources:

- Brands
- Systems
- Capital and, most important,
- People

Because these resources are already available, one might assume we need only to draw on them for achieving our goal. Nothing could be more wrong. The challenge of the 1990s will be not only to use these resources, but to expand them . . . to adapt them . . . to reconfigure them in constantly changing ways in order to bring about an ever renewed relationship between the Coca-Cola system and the consumers of the world . . . to make the best even better.

Our resources
BRANDS   Increasing globalization of the communications industry means we can more effectively expose our advertising and other image-building programs through a worldwide brand framework. This places a premium on maintaining our traditional excellence as premier brand advertiser. Yet, we must remember that it is our franchisee network around the world which will distribute and locally market our brands. To appropriately leverage these brands, we must recognize that we and our franchisees are fundamentally in the business of servicing our customers and meeting the needs, real or perceived, of our customers.

Tactical decisions regarding the marketing of our products must stay as close to the customer and consumer as possible, within a clear, but flexible, global brand strategy. This is another way of saying that we must think globally but act locally. Thus, intimate knowledge of an account, a channel, or a consumer segment will be required to design specific programs which generate satisfaction and value to that customer or consumer. The Coca-Cola Company does not sell commodities – we will not sell commodities – and we will not cheapen our relationships with customers and consumers.

Coca-Cola, in every form . . . classic, diet, caffeine free, cherry, light . . . is the most widely recognized and esteemed brand in the world. Coca-Cola was, is, and always will be . . . it! It is the centerpiece of our entire refreshment system.

Sprite and Fanta are worldwide brands. They must play a role in our brand strategy. We will continually strive to develop new brands where the opportunity presents itself.

SYSTEMS   Moving closer to the consumer both in our own organizational structure and in timely decision-making will be mandated by the global, yet diverse, marketplace of the 1990s.

Structurally, a flatter organization of our Company will be required. Functional groups must be reorganized around business units which focus on market opportunities. And as a company, we must be players, not just cheerleaders or critics.

It will be essential that our franchisees understand this new role we see for ourselves. Our increased equity participation in the Coca-Cola production and distribution network, which may include complete franchise consolidations in some areas of the world, will be carried out *only* whenever it becomes necessary for achieving our goal. A greater involvement in our franchise system will likely necessitate our making investments to help bring about production and distribution capabilities which meet the service demands of customers at the lowest possible cost. This is to ensure a competitive advantage for the entire system.

Entirely new distribution systems may be needed to realize new opportunities in vending and in new and emerging post-mix markets, particularly outside the United States. Joint ventures, in many forms, with our franchisees and suppliers will put our capital directly into building new avenues to reach consumers.

Success in managing these flatter, market-driven structures will depend largely on our information systems. To reach our goal, our information systems – the processes, reports, procedures, and communication linkages that hold the organization together – must lead, rather than trail, developments in the marketplace. Effective and timely information is vital to effective and timely allocation of resources.

Ours is a multi-local business. Its relative state of development varies dramatically from the soft drink frontiers of Asia to the sophisticated markets of North America. Throughout our 103-year history there has been an evolutionary process or cycle of development continuously at work. That cycle, which often evolved over decades in the past, will quicken in astonishing dimensions in the future. By the year 2000, our business system in developing countries must function at levels nearly equal to those seen in today's sophisticated markets. Where lack of hard currency or difficult political realities are constraints to reaching consumers, we must build new strategic alliances and enhance our trading capabilities to overcome constraints.

CAPITAL   Shaping business systems which are close to consumers will require not only the investment of our capital for new assets, but more sophisticated management of existing ones. Existing assets will be evaluated as potential resources for meeting our goal. Those assets include not only physical assets but also equity ownership positions, financial capacity, and information systems, as well as creative management of key business relationships.

Capital management is no longer just the process of earning a rate of return above our cost of capital. It is the innovative endeavor of finding more productive uses and new purposes for assets, of trading or leveraging existing assets to meet our goal and to create new strategic alliances.

Our organization has a rich history of effectively allocating resources and of utilizing our financial strength to build value. That will continue. And given our growing experience at managing greater financial leverage, we will periodically evaluate higher leverage ceilings, primarily for investments in our business system or in strategic alliances and, secondarily, in our own shares.

PEOPLE   Through the years, the Coca-Cola Company has always had an international cadre of individuals. To capture the global soft drink opportunity in the 1990s, we need more than the right brands, systems, and infrastructure. We need the right people for the 21st century.

We must have people who use facts and knowledge to add something ... to add value to our customers' businesses. In an age where everyone has basically the same information at the same time, the advantage goes to people who can take information and quickly put it to effective and profitable use. It means having people with what can be called the 'mind of the strategist' . . . people who can create a competitive advantage . . . out of common knowledge.

Few are born with such skill. This skill can be developed, however, and should be rewarded. We must recruit and nurture the growth of associates to match the needs to the business. In the 1990s 'internationalists' with multilingual, multicultural capabilities will be the norm. And we must continue to refine our compensation systems to reflect our operating culture and reward value-adding performance.

The responsibility for developing people cannot be delegated to training courses, academic exercises, or professionals in the area of human resources. Those have a role to play but do not constitute an adequate process. The development of our best people is the personal responsibility of Management. It requires each manager to see his or her most important responsibility as teaching and developing people. Our charge is simple – recruiting and training the best talent by the best managers. As that talent grows and develops, they become the next managers capable of and responsible for developing new talent, thus perpetuating a strength.

This process is the link to maintaining the sense of dissatisfaction that has resulted in much of the success we enjoy today. We must continue to cultivate intelligent risk-taking and flexible decision-making, realizing that while not every risk taken or decision made brings success, the alternative is complacency and stagnation ... a stance totally unacceptable to our Company.

Our rewards
The rewards of meeting these challenges and flourishing in a state of rapid change are enormous:

- Satisfied consumers who return again and again to our brands for refreshment;
- Communities around the world where we are an economic contributor and welcomed guest;
- Successful business partners; and
- Shareholders who are building value through the power of the Coca-Cola system.

Our shared vision
The Coca-Cola system is indeed a special business. One hundred and three years of dedicated effort by literally millions of individuals have combined to create in Coca-Cola a remarkable trademark presence and economic value unchallenged since the dawn of commercial history.

However, any edge we have is fragile. Our journey to the year 2000 requires that our brands, systems, capital and people grow and change to meet our goal and thus realize our opportunity. To borrow a recent popular phrase, we see six billion points of light in a thirsty world – six billion consumers in the world of the year 2000 – all being refreshed as never before by the Coca-Cola system.

That is a wonderful goal we all can share and strive for as we move together – toward 2000.

---

24 Coopers & Lybrand USA   Accountants

"Solutions for business"

Our mission is to be the leading business advisers.

---

25 Dalgety plc UK   Foods

Dalgety is a major food group with leading positions in snackfoods, petfoods, grocery products, food ingredients, food distribution and agribusiness.

Our strategy is to build on the strengths of our core business by investing in areas where we see potential for strong, sustainable growth in earnings.

We recruit and retain high quality people, providing them with clear strategic and financial parameters within which to make their own day-to-day management decisions.

We play a responsible role in the communities in which we work, whilst seeking to provide our shareholders with increased earnings, our customers with high quality products and services and our employees with rewarding careers.

---

26   Dana Corporation   Automotive
USA

Mission statement: ten key thoughts

- Dana people serve the shareholder
- Dana people are our most important asset
- Dana people accept only total quality
- Dana people discourage centralization
- Dana people do what's best for all of Dana
- Dana people participate and innovate
- Dana people compete globally
- Dana people focus on the customer
- Dana people communicate fully
- Dana people are good citizens

---

27   DHL Worldwide Express   Air couriers
USA/Belgium

"We keep your promises"

Worldwide mission statement
DHL will become the acknowledged global leader in the express delivery of documents and packages. Leadership will be achieved by establishing the industry standards of excellence for quality of service and by maintaining the lowest cost position relative to our service commitment in all markets of the world.

Achievement of the mission requires:
Absolute dedication to understanding and fulfilling our customers' needs with the appropriate mix of service, reliability, products and price for each customer.

An environment that rewards achievement, enthusiasm, and team spirit and which offers each person in DHL superior opportunities for personal development and growth.

A state-of-the-art worldwide information network for customer billing, tracking, tracing and management information/communications.

Allocation of resources consistent with the recognition that we are one worldwide business.

A professional organisation able to maintain local initiative and local decision-making while working together within a centrally managed network.

The evolution of our business into new services, markets, or products will be completely driven by our single-minded commitment to anticipating and meeting the changing needs of our customers.

---

28   Du Pont   Chemicals
USA

"Better things for better living, through chemistry"

Our mission . . .
Du Pont is a diversified chemical, energy and specialty products company with a strong tradition of discovery. Our global businesses are constantly evolving and continually searching for new and better ways to use our human, technological and financial resources to improve the quality of life of people around the world.

The mission that drives us is ongoing and challenging . . . to increase the value of the company to customers, employees and shareholders by profitably providing beneficial products and services to worldwide markets.

In doing so, each of our businesses must deliver financial results superior to those of its leading competitors . . . for we consider ourselves successful only if we return to our shareholders a long-term financial reward comparable to the better performing, large industrial companies.

While much of our growth occurs through discovery and development of new products, energy resources and services, our success depends ultimately upon our total commitment to serving the needs of the marketplace. This requires that we work in full partnership with our customers . . . not only in understanding and meeting customer needs, but in anticipating their problems as well.

Above all, we recognize that the degree of our success is in direct proportion to the quality and dedication of our people.

To be more successful than our competitors, we must never be satisfied with the status quo . . . we must be calculated risk takers with a compulsive curiosity . . . curiosity to seek the most innovative answers to the most complex problems . . . bringing better things for better living to the marketplace.

Our principles . . .
A significant factor contributing to our success is adherence to a distinctive set of guiding principles and commonly shared values.

Customer orientation
We must focus our energies on customers and markets, constantly striving for excellence in understanding, anticipating and serving their needs faster and better than our competitors.

Competitive position
We must serve those markets in which we can be the best . . . markets where our human, technological and financial strengths give us opportunities to establish and maintain leadership positions and achieve profitable growth. Further, we must be aggressive in both acquiring and divesting businesses to enhance those positions.

Management style
We must manage our diverse businesses with organizational structures, systems and policies that enable them to excel in the markets they serve. In so doing, calculated risk taking must be encouraged to maximize returns, and barriers that inhibit achievement of full business and individual potential eliminated.

Individual opportunity
We must treat each other fairly, with respect for individual dignity, while developing our talents and skills to their full potential to increase our contributions to the success of the businesses we serve. Our recognition, rewards and advancement must be based on the value of those contributions as we strive for continuous improvement in the quality of everything we do.

Ethical behavior
We must conduct our business affairs with the highest ethical standards and work diligently to be a respected corporate citizen worldwide.

Safety
We must adhere to the highest standards for the safe operation of facilities and the protection of the environment, our people and customers, and the citizens of the communities in which we do business.

---

29   Elswick plc   Engineering
UK   products manufacturer

Elswick business philosophy

- The customer provides our livelihood
- Only top quality is good enough
- We aspire to be an ethical company
- We believe people matter
- There is no substitute for the facts
- We want to keep on growing
- We look outwards
- We want to do today what others do tomorrow

The Elswick Emblem formed by a four-fold letter 'E', not

only underlines the name but is intended to signify the Elswick approach to doing business:

<u>E – Enterprise</u>
We seek to encourage an entrepreneurial attitude enabling enterprising developments to flourish.

<u>E – Energy</u>
We apply our combined energy to enterprising development so as to produce positive action.

<u>E – Effectiveness</u>
We believe that management's task is to convert positive action into effective achievement of our aims and objectives.

<u>E – Enthusiasm</u>
An enthusiastic attitude is the lubricant of our combined efforts to be enterprising, energetic and effective in the conduct of our business.

---

30 Factors Chain International   Association
The Netherlands

"FCI: The <u>standard</u> in international factoring"

FCI is a global network of leading factoring companies, whose common aim is to facilitate international trade through factoring and related financial services.

FCI's mission is to become the worldwide standard for international factoring.

FCI helps its members achieve competitive advantage in international trade finance services through:

- A global network of first-class factoring companies
- Modern and effective communication systems, to enable them to conduct their business in a cost-efficient way
- A reliable legal framework to protect exporters and importers
- Standard procedures aimed at maintaining a universal quality

- A package of training programs
- Worldwide promotion aimed at positioning international factoring as the preferred method of trade finance

FCI will always have a flexible and market-oriented attitude. It will remain an open chain, encouraging quality factoring companies to join its ranks. As an open chain, FCI will view competition as a stimulus for superior service to exporters.

FCI: The *standard* in international factoring.

---

31   Federal Express   Air couriers
USA

"When it absolutely, positively, has to be there on time"

Our corporate mission
Federal Express is committed to our PEOPLE–SERVICE–PROFIT philosophy. We will produce outstanding financial returns by providing totally reliable, competitively superior, global air–ground transportation of high priority goods and documents that require rapid, time-certain delivery. Equally important, positive control of each package will be maintained utilizing real-time electronic tracking and tracing systems. A complete record of each shipment and delivery will be presented with our request for payment. We will be helpful, courteous and professional to each other and the public. We will strive to have a completely satisfied customer at the end of each transaction.

Federal Express strategy
Federal Express puts great emphasis on strategy. We have a very succinct corporate mission. Our concentration in the field of high-priority logistics is the result of considerable study and deliberation by the senior management team.

Each member of the Federal Express management team must be keenly aware of these various influences and, even more importantly, the highly focused strategy that we have adopted. The understanding of both the process of strategy development and our particular strategy provides a road map for the manager. Sharing these Corporate values, thousands of managerial personnel can concentrate their efforts towards the same objectives.

Our strategy has two underlying themes. First, we believe in the requirement to differentiate our services from those of our competitors to maintain our leadership position and to produce superior financial returns. Secondly, we offer only high-value-added services. Our high-priority logistic markets require outstanding performance by outstanding people, so this insistence on pursuing high-value-added opportunities is extremely important to our customer franchise. And only by engaging in those activities that are hard to do – where considerable value is added by the supplier – can Federal Express provide outstanding opportunities, wages and benefits to our employer group. Professor Theodore Levitt of the Harvard Business School addressed both of these issues in his book, *The Marketing Imagination*, when he noted that:

'People buy products (whether purely tangible products, purely intangible products or hybrids of the two) in order to solve problems. Products are problem-solving tools. The product is (to the potential buyer) a complete cluster of value satisfactions.'

Levitt goes on to note that differentiating your product offerings is essential in communicating to your customers that their problems can best be solved by your company. If distinguishing features of product differentiation are absent, customers will choose either randomly or based on non-business criteria.

Corporate strengths
Over the last several years as competition in our traditional markets has increased and the risk of technological change has affected our strategies, we have developed a strategy based on an objective appraisal of our Corporate strengths. These are the Corporate strengths of Federal Express:

- We have enormous aviation skills
- We have substantial technical expertise in electronics
- We have an outstanding brand name and an excellent reputation for service as demonstrated by winning the Malcolm Baldridge National Quality Award
- We have extensive worldwide distribution and telecommunications networks
- We have a strong presence in all major international markets
- We have an outstanding group of employees who are superior to the workforces with whom we compete

We have formulated our strategic goals based on these Corporate strengths, and we have deliberately avoided competing in those areas that do not first lend themselves to our twin strategic tenets of product differentiation and high value added or, secondly, that do not play to our Corporate strengths.

Federal Express's strategic objectives/critical success factors
These strategic objectives/critical success factors are derived from our Corporate mission and strategic tenets [proprietary detail omitted]:

- Continuously improve quality to achieve 100% on-time deliveries, 100% information accuracy and 100% customer satisfaction after every contact with Federal Express
- Lower costs and prices
- Make international profitable and the world's leading express system
- Get closer to our customers
- Continue to focus on People – Service – Profit issues

Federal Express's strategy is a strength in its own right. The enormous energy represented by the motivated workforce and management group making up the Federal Express team is capable of incredible accomplishment if efforts are concentrated. To capitalize on the full potential of this concentrated source of energy, all managers and their employees must understand and support our strategic objectives.

---

32   Ford Motor Company Ltd   Cars
UK

"Everything we do is driven by you"

Company statement on mission, values and guiding principles

Mission
Ford Motor Company is a worldwide leader in automotive and automotive-related products and services as well as in newer industries such as aerospace, communications and financial services. Our mission is to improve continually our products and services to meet our customers' needs, allowing us to prosper as a business and to provide a reasonable return for our stockholders, the owners of our business.

Values
How we accomplish our mission is as important as the mission itself. Fundamental to success for the Company are these basic values:

People – Our people are the source of our strength. They provide our corporate intelligence and determine our reputation and vitality. Involvement and teamwork are our core human values.

Products – Our products are the end result of our efforts, and they should be the best in serving customers worldwide. As our products are viewed, so are we viewed.

Profits – Our profits are the ultimate measure of how efficiently we provide customers with the best products for their needs. Profits are required to survive and grow.

Guiding principles
Quality comes first – To achieve customer satisfaction, the

quality of our products and services must be our number one priority.

Customers are the focus of everything we do – Our work must be done with our customers in mind, providing better products and services than our competition.

Continuous improvement is essential to our success – We must strive for excellence in everything we do: in our products, in their safety and value – and in our services, our human relations, our competitiveness and our profitability.

Employee involvement is our way of life – We are a team. We must treat each other with trust and respect.

Dealers and suppliers are our partners – The Company must maintain mutually beneficial relationships with dealers, suppliers and our other business associates.

Integrity is never compromised – The conduct of our Company worldwide must be pursued in a manner that is socially responsible and commands respect for its integrity and for its positive contributions to society. Our doors are open to men and women alike without discrimination and without regard to ethnic origin or personal beliefs.

---

33   Forte plc   UK   Hotels and catering

"Host to the world"

Our company philosophy

To increase profitability and earnings per share each year in order to encourage investment and to improve and expand the business

To give complete customer satisfaction by efficient and courteous service, with value for money

To support managers and their staff in using personal initiative to improve the profit and quality of their operations whilst observing the Company's policies

To provide good working conditions and to maintain effective communications at all levels to develop better understanding and assist decision-making

To ensure no discrimination against sex, race, colour or creed

To train, develop and encourage promotion within the Company based on merit and ability

To act with integrity and to maintain a proper sense of responsibility towards the public

To recognise the importance of each and every employee

---

34   Gallaher Ltd UK   Diversified consumer

Gallaher Ltd is a major international group based in the UK. The Group is an autonomous subsidiary of American Brands, Inc. Gallaher's business interests span tobacco, distilled spirits, optical, retail distribution and housewares. The Group owns a wide portfolio of successful, strongly branded goods and services in each of these areas.

The creation and development of individual brands is central to the Group's philosophy. Tobacco brands such as Benson & Hedges, Silk Cut, Berkeley, Hamlet and Condor lead their respective market sectors in the UK. Similarly, Gallaher's success in other sectors is founded upon well-known and well-respected names such as Whyte & Mackay, Dollond & Aitchison, Forbuoys and Prestige.

Exports – particularly to European markets – form a large and increasingly important part of Gallaher's business. From an exceptionally strong tobacco base, Gallaher operates a policy of selective diversification, choosing only those companies which correspond to its own high standards in terms of UK and European growth prospects, and management efficacy and skill.

In order to attain these standards, the Group invests in the single most valuable asset it possesses: its people. From top quality management training programmes to the emphasis placed on teamwork throughout the Group, Gallaher encourages excellence. The Group has a long tradition of concern for staff welfare and is committed to a policy of equal opportunities.

Gallaher aims to secure consistent, profitable growth across all areas of its operations. Following the tradition set by its founder in 1857, the Group seeks to maintain the reputation for quality for which its people and products are renowned.

---

35 The General Electric Company plc Electrical UK

- At GEC, we will do our utmost to provide value and high standards of service to customers and will encourage our suppliers to do the same.
- We will play a constructive role in the communities in which our facilities are established, paying due regard to environmental considerations.
- We will encourage and reward the productivity and ingenuity of the people who work in the Company.
- We will ensure our technological leadership by maintaining excellent research and development staff and providing them with the facilities they need.
- We will continue to exercise the style of management which has been proven over many years.
- We will achieve profitable growth from within the company, through imaginative management of our assets.
- We will encourage further growth through acquisition, partnerships, joint ventures and technical collaboration.
- We will seek to maximise the value of our shareholders' investment by consistently raising earnings per share while maintaining prudent accounting standards.

---

36   Girl Guides Association   Association
UK

Its purpose is to enable girls to mature into confident, capable and caring women determined, as individuals, to realise their potential in their career, home and personal life, and willing, as citizens, to contribute to their community and the wider world.

---

37   GKN plc   Engineering
UK

Corporate statement

GKN is an international group of companies with annual sales of some £2500 million, designing, developing and manufacturing automotive components and other engineered products and providing a range of industrial and distribution services.

Our aims are to:

- Provide our customers with high quality and competitively priced products and services
- Provide our shareholders with growing returns on their investment
- Continue to develop and grow the Group in its chosen business areas by acquisition and investment
- Provide our employees with job satisfaction and the opportunity for personal development
- Contribute to the communities and safeguard the environment in which we operate
- Manage our business with integrity

GKN values

- Quality is our first priority. We must look for quality in our products and services, in our working practices and in our human relationships – with our customers, with our suppliers, with the communities in which we work and with each other. We must pursue excellence and continuous improvement in everything we do.

- Our people are our greatest strength. It is their vitality, commitment and skill which provide the foundations for our continued success. We will build on this strength by encouraging teamwork and employee involvement and by providing opportunities for continuous learning and development matched to individual abilities and the needs of our business. We support the principle of equal opportunity irrespective of sex, race, colour or creed.

- Wherever we are in the world, we must understand the regulatory framework within which we work and our conduct must be of the highest order. We must act with integrity at all times. Our business ethics must never be compromised and we expect the highest personal standards to be maintained by our employees. We are also conscious of our social responsibilities and expect to make a positive contribution to those communities in which we operate, both local and national.

- The financial well-being of the Group is a fundamental requirement. Our profitability is a measure of our success, both in meeting the needs of our customers and in the efficient management of our business. Profits are vital to our development and growth and to the increase in value of our shareholders' investment.

---

38 Glaxo Holdings plc   Pharmaceuticals
UK

"World leaders in pharmaceuticals"

Glaxo is an integrated research-based group of companies whose corporate purpose is the discovery, development, manufacture and marketing of safe, effective medicines of the highest quality.

---

39   Glynwed plc   Metals
UK

Glynwed is a major processor of metals and plastics, providing a vital link between producers of basic materials and manu-facturers of countless finished products.

With leading brands of its own, Glynwed also creates quality in finished products for the home and for industry.

Through its distribution of metals and plastics, Glynwed delivers value in specialist materials to a multiplicity of cus-tomers worldwide.

---

40   Heidrick & Struggles International Inc
USA   Executive search

Executive search is our profession. The search to find out-standing executives for our clients; in whichever industry or sector they operate, and wherever they may be based. This has been our profession for more than 35 years. At first throughout North America, and now across Europe and the Pacific Basin, we are dedicated to excellence and success in our consulting work. Our fundamental commitment in every assignment we undertake is: 'To identify and attract executives of the highest possible calibre who will enhance the value of our clients' business.'

---

41   Hepworth plc   Diversified
UK

Hepworth is a major European group with five divisions.

In each of the Group's main areas of activity strong market positions have been achieved through innovative marketing, low cost manufacturing and strict financial disciplines.

Management of the Group is decentralised and considerable autonomy is given to divisional managements.

The Group's strategy is to grow through a combination of

organic growth and acquisitions in areas of known expertise with particular emphasis on continental Europe.

---

42   Hertz (UK) Ltd   Car rental
UK

"You don't just rent a car, you rent a company"

Quality policy
Hertz (UK) Ltd makes a quality of service commitment to *all* its customers. This ongoing commitment is supported by the Hertz (UK) quality declaration:

Vision
To provide a level of service that *never* fails, but meets our customers' needs every time.

'Satisfied customers are our greatest asset'

Mission
Exceed our customers' expectations by delivering *the* rental experience that is second to none.

'Get it right first time, every time'

Policy
Through the process of a formally documented quality plan, monitor every stage of our service production to ensure continual improvement of our standards.

---

43   Hillsdown plc   Food
UK

Hillsdown is a leading international food group with substantial interests in Europe and North America.

Fundamental to Hillsdown's success is its policy of:

- Building major market shares with strong customer relationships
- Owning a balanced portfolio of quality products
- Investing in its business to ensure efficient low cost production and increasing margins
- Developing a well-motivated and decentralised management
- Making timely acquisitions and disposals.

---

44 Honda Motor Company   Cars
Japan

"Progress with distinction"

Company principle
Maintaining an international viewpoint, we are dedicated to supplying products of the highest efficiency at a reasonable price for worldwide customer satisfaction.

Management policy

1. Proceed always with ambition and youthfulness.
2. Respect sound theory, develop fresh ideas and make the most effective use of time.
3. Enjoy your work and always brighten your working atmosphere.
4. Strive constantly for a harmonious flow of work.
5. Be ever mindful of the value of research and endeavour.

---

45 Hunting plc   Industrial
UK

Hunting plc is an Industrial Holding Company. Its subsidiaries operate internationally within three divisions: Defence, Aviation and Oil.

Its aim is to maximise value for shareholders through growth in profits and earnings by focusing on those activities where its skills and resources can achieve the maximum benefit.

---

46   IBM UK Ltd   Computers
UK

"I think, therefore IBM"

IBM UK is responsible for the short-term management and long-term optimisation of the IBM Corporation's business within and from the UK in a balanced manner, which also:

1. Fulfils IBM's basic beliefs of:
   - Respect for the individual
   - Service to the customer
   - Pursuit of excellence
2. Establishes us as a market-driven company.
3. Meets the Corporation's business goals to:
   - Enhance our customer partnerships
   - Be the leader in products and services (provide solutions which excel in quality and innovation)
   - Grow with the industry
   - Be the most efficient in everything we do
   - Sustain our profitability (which funds our future growth)
4. Gives proper regard to meeting the needs of the other stakeholders:
   - Business associates
   - The community

---

47 Imperial Chemical Industries plc   Chemicals
UK

"World problems. World solutions. World class."

The chemical industry is a major force for the improvement of the quality of life across the world. ICI aims to be the world's leading chemical company, serving customers internationally through the innovative and responsible application of chemistry and related sciences.

Through achievement of our aim, we will enhance the wealth and well-being of our shareholders, our employees, our customers and the communities which we serve and in which we operate.

We will do this by:

- Seeking consistent profitable growth;
- Providing challenge and opportunity for our employees, releasing their skills and creativity;
- Achieving a standard of quality and service internationally which our customers recognise as being consistently better than that of any of our competitors;
- Operating safely and in harmony with the global environment.

---

48 Inchcape plc   Business services
UK

Our mission is to be the world's premier international services and marketing group and to provide outstanding shareholder value.

---

49   Jaguar Cars Ltd   Cars
UK

"What are dreams for if not to come true?"

Quality policy and mission statement

Mission
Jaguar's heritage is founded on a long history of distinctive cars which offered a unique blend of style, performance, refinement, prestige and affordability.

We aim to build on this tradition, ensuring that current and future Jaguars provide the highest standard of driving pleasure and ownership satisfaction.

We must deliver this with world-class standards of quality and operating efficiency in order to offer our customers outstanding value for money.

In this way we can generate the profits required to secure the future of the Company, its employees, dealers and suppliers.

Goals
Products: To produce the best cars in the world, ensuring that every component part:

- is based on a design which emphasises quality;
- comes from a quality supplier;
- is thoroughly tested before introduction; and
- is produced on a proven manufacturing process.

People: To provide competitive, secure, long-term employment, in an environment of mutual trust, courtesy and respect.

Profits: To satisfy our customers efficiently, thereby generating profits to ensure survival and growth.

Growth: To fully exploit the growth potential of the Jaguar marque and heritage.

Operating principles

The way we manage and operate is as important as the achievement of specific goals. The following principles apply to all operations:

- That quality, defined as exceeding customers' internal or external requirements, be the prime consideration in any decision or action.

- That every work process be examined compared with customer requirements and improved using statistical methods to reduce variability.

- That management seek out and remove every barrier to pride of workmanship and take every measure to make it possible for all employees to dedicate themselves to the future of the Company with confidence.

- That every employee be expected to participate in the continuous improvement of every operation. Jaguar accepts the responsibility in providing the training and leadership to make the participation effective.

- That our suppliers, dealers and trade unions be encouraged to share our commitment to total customer satisfaction.

- That we are socially responsible and conduct our business with integrity.

---

50   John Laing plc UK   Construction

"We care and it shows"

John Laing plc is a major force in the construction, housing, mechanical engineering and technology related markets in the UK with operations in a growing number of overseas markets.

The Group's successful and flexible blend of services, skills and products is tailored to meet the needs of each individual client, and is complemented by its continuing caring concern for the community, the environment and its own employees and pensioners.

The Group's strategy remains to build on its strengths. It continues to focus on the core businesses of Construction and Homes, developing its ancillary skills and activities to support them.

In parallel there is a continued drive to increase the productivity, efficiency and cost-consciousness of all parts of the Group, and to maintain the proven high standards of quality, safety and reliability to the benefit of customers, shareholders and employees.

---

51 John Menzies Group plc   Retailing
UK

Our endeavour
To operate successfully and develop dominant businesses in retailing and in distribution services.

To provide the highest quality of goods and services to our customers, both corporate and individual.

To carry out our business with the highest standards of integrity.

To contribute wherever possible to the welfare and quality of life of the community.

To maintain real growth in earnings per share, at a better than average sector rate, in the long-term interest of our staff and shareholders.

To retain the existing concentration of share ownership.

---

52 Johnson & Johnson   Pharmaceuticals
USA

Our credo
We believe our first responsibility is to the doctors, nurses and patients, to mothers and fathers and all others who use our products and services. In meeting their needs everything we do must be of high quality. We must constantly strive to reduce our costs in order to maintain reasonable

prices. Customers' orders must be serviced promptly and accurately. Our suppliers and distributors must have an opportunity to make a fair profit.

We are responsible to our employees, the men and women who work with us throughout the world. Everyone must be considered as an individual. We must respect their dignity and recognize their merit. They must have a sense of security in their jobs. Compensation must be fair and adequate, and working conditions clean, orderly and safe. We must be mindful of ways to help our employees fulfill their family responsibilities. Employees must feel free to make suggestions and complaints. There must be equal opportunity for employment, development and advancement for those qualified. We must provide competent management, and their actions must be just and ethical.

We are responsible to the communities in which we live and work and to the world community as well. We must be good citizens – support good works and charities and bear our fair share of taxes. We must encourage civic improvements and better health and education. We must maintain in good order the property we are privileged to use, protecting the environment and natural resources.

Our final responsibility is to our stockholders. Business must make a sound profit. We must experiment with new ideas. Research must be carried on, innovative programs developed and mistakes paid for. New equipment must be purchased, new facilities provided and new products launched. Reserves must be created to provide for adverse times. When we operate according to these principles, the stockholders should realize a fair return.

---

53 Kleinwort Benson Group plc   Merchant
UK   banking

An independent European merchant bank, based in London and operating selectively elsewhere.

Our vision is:
By helping clients to prosper, to build our business profitably.

Our aims are:
To promote the long-term development of our merchant banking franchise and reputation; and to provide superior returns to our shareholders and competitive rewards for our employees.

---

54 Koninklijke (Royal) Ahold NV   Foods
The Netherlands

Corporate principles
Ahold is primarily a retail organization, distributing and producing consumer goods, and rendering services directly to large numbers of customers directly through its chain-stores in the Netherlands, other countries in Europe, and the United States.

The objective of the company is to continue to perform this role in society in current as well as in new market areas, and, by doing so, to achieve a proper return on investment, while at the same time providing substantial employment.

To achieve its objective and meet its related responsibilities, the company needs to ensure its continuity. Ahold wishes to be able to determine its own future, and therefore strives to maintain its independence and its own identity.

The consumer is at the very heart of Ahold's policy. Consequently, Ahold monitors the desires of the consumer and the ever-changing market conditions. Here, the basic principle is to give consumers value for money, and at the same time devote a great deal of attention to quality, assortment, safety and information.

For its employees, Ahold wants to be a company that not only offers adequate compensation, but also provides challenges, professional training, education and motivation.

For the stockholders, Ahold aims at a good return on investment. All new and existing activities will be continually tested against this criterion. Ahold makes an effort to inform interested parties, as often as is possible and justifiable, of the course of events in the company.

Ahold strives for a steady relationship with its suppliers that meets the commercial interests of both parties. Social concerns like employment, zoning and planning, environment and public health will be important elements of corporate policy.

---

55   Kwik Save Group plc   Food retailing
UK

"It makes good sense"

Our charter

- The more efficiently we operate the more our customers benefit from the best prices.

- We only sell top brands and top sellers – we never compromise on quality.

- We always use our buying power to obtain the keenest costs and pass on the savings through our everyday low prices.

- We operate smaller, efficient stores that are conveniently located and easy to shop in.

- We don't insult our customers with frills or gimmicks for which, ultimately, they have to pay.

We believe that all this adds up to the best value grocery shopping in the United Kingdom.

---

56   The Leigh Group   Environmental services
UK

Our mission statement
The purpose of this statement is to identify to shareholders,

employees, customers and suppliers, and the world at large the unchanging principles on which our business is conducted and by which our performance may be judged.

It is displayed in all our offices and will be printed in major items of company literature.

Leigh pioneered waste management in the UK. Its goal is to remain the leading independent British company wholly dedicated to this activity, making use of its capabilities both nationally and internationally.

Leigh earns the livelihood of its employees and the return on its shareholders' investment through the management and treatment of the waste produced by mankind.

It collects waste from where it arises and transports it safely to plants and sites where it is licensed to deal with it, aiming to be as good a neighbour as the excellence of its technology and the responsibility of its employees can make it.

In all its activities, its policy is to act in a socially responsible way and ultimately to improve the quality of the environment, leaving it a better place than it was when Leigh found it.

---

57   Lever Brothers Ltd   Fast-moving
UK   consumer goods

Overall objective
Our overall objective is to maximise the inherent value of the business – its ability to generate profit flows – which is what the owners of the business, our shareholders, self-evidently seek.

Mission
We intend to become and to remain the most successful cleaning, care and hygiene business in the world ('successful' is used to mean economic efficiency, measured by greater, long-term profitability).

We shall achieve this superiority over competitors because we shall better understand the consumers of our products and thus be better able to forecast and meet their needs. We shall also better understand the requirements of our trade customers. Consequently, we shall develop, design, manufacture, market and distribute most economically the products that they desire. This will yield scale advantage that we shall exploit throughout the world.

Our business must combine two antithetic qualities – an overall robustness that is proof against hostile or adverse forces; and an attitude towards risk-taking that encourages initiatives.

Responsibilities

We shall conduct all aspects of our business in a responsible manner:

- We shall never intentionally damage the environment in which we operate, nor put at risk our consumers, nor our people;
- We shall strive to give our people a just share in the business's success, to give them proper authority and the opportunity for individual fulfilment, and to treat them fairly; we must be seen to recognise merit, integrity and achievement;
- It goes without saying that we shall, of course, deal honestly and openly with consumers of our brands; and fairly and professionally with our trade customers and suppliers;
- We shall play a responsible part in the communities in which we operate, respecting their customs and obeying their laws.

Other objectives and policies

1. We shall become the leading industrial detergents business in the world.
2. Given the maturity of our detergent business, we should produce better than Concern-target yields and cash flows.
3. We shall conduct our operations by means of consumer-preferred brands which are continually updated and

improved. R&D and innovation from all sources are vital to our success in this objective. Product quality is of prime importance.

4. We seek lowest-cost operation by achieving maximum scale advantage. Thus in Europe, Lever will be run as a European business wherever this is advantageous, using the combined skills of total European management to seek optimum European profit performance. Lowest-cost operation implies elimination of waste, defined as cost that produces nothing that the consumer values.

5. Our work is self-evidently a team effort and this must be apparent in our organisational practices. Only if we harness the combined intelligence and imagination of our people shall we succeed.

6. We have rejected two out-dated organisational concepts – centralism or head office direction and complete devolution of responsibility to companies. We use a system best described as 'networking' – bringing to bear on our problems a network of management skill and experience, some located centrally, some located in various companies, all focused on the goal of European optimisation.

7. Our decisions will always be rational. We must always be in a position to explain them.

8. We are in business forever. We put our long-term interests before the short-term and our work method will be based upon long-term strategies and plans.

Conclusion

Our mission says that we shall be more successful than competitors, and that needs some justification.

The things that make our business distinctive – its people, its history, its standards, its known success, its known objectives, its multinationality – are precisely the qualities which make it possible for our people to achieve more for themselves and for us than they could in any other business. Thus shall we be more successful than our competitors.

58 Libbey-Owens-Ford   Glass
   USA

Vision

We want Libbey-Owens-Ford to become a thriving and prosperous company where every person can make their life better and the company the recognized leader in the markets we serve.

Beliefs

We believe we must have an every-minute-of-the-day obsession with satisfying all of our customers' needs and expectations.

We believe we must continually improve our quality – the quality of our products, the quality of our service, and the quality of the way we do things.

We believe we must create a workplace where people have the room and tools to grow and shape their own work experience.

Commitment

This is a commitment to our customers, to our company, to ourselves and to the needs of the future we face.

---

59 Lloyds Bank plc   Banking
   UK

"The thoroughbred bank"

Our aim is to be the best and most successful company in the financial services industry – best in customer service, best to work for, best in creating value for our shareholders. But superior performance does not come easily.

We have many able competitors and more to come in the years ahead. To be the best, we know that we must have the best people, backed by the best technology and the best training, and concentrate their efforts on those businesses in which we have the experience and ability to excel.

Our strategy starts with our customers. We can only create value for our shareholders if we create value for our customers. And customers' needs and expectations are changing rapidly. Today's customers are more selective than ever. They want wider choice. They want better quality. Above all, they want greater value for money. That is why our strategy is to focus on the things we can do well and then strive to do them better than anybody else.

The successful management of change is crucial to our progress. We see innovation – whether in the form of a better product, service or delivery system or a lower cost product, service or delivery system – as the main way to encourage people to buy from us instead of our competitors. To attract and hold our share of customers, we have to adjust to their changing needs, not expect them to adapt to ours.

---

60   London Business School   Education
UK

To be a world leader in helping individuals and organisations enhance their managerial effectiveness.

To do so by pursuing a balanced excellence that links theory to practice in teaching and research that are innovative, rigorous and relevant to international, career-long learning.

---

61   Marion Merrell Dow Inc   Pharmaceuticals

Global corporate mission statement
To be the best global pharmaceutical company at improving the longevity and/or quality of human life.

Core. Through excellence in the fulfillment of customer needs, Marion Merrell Dow will attain global market leadership in prescription and over-the-counter products.

Environment. Providing our associates with a performance-oriented, safe working environment that stimulates integrity, entrepreneurial spirit, productivity and a sense of social responsibility.

Science. Assuring new-product continuity through innovative internal discovery research and the aggressive pursuit of external licensing, acquisition and research opportunities.

Quality. Striving for continuous measurable improvement in all functions and elements of our company to provide a level of quality in our products and services that sets the standard for the industry.

Profitability. Achieving a continuum of profitable growth that ranks us among the industry leaders.

---

62 Marks & Spencer   Retailing
UK

Company principles
Selling clothing for the family, homeware, and a range of fine foods – all representing high standards of quality and value.

Creating an attractive, efficient shopping environment for customers.

Providing a friendly, helpful service from well-trained staff.

Sharing mutually beneficial, long-term partnerships with suppliers, who use modern and efficient production techniques.

Supporting British industry and buying abroad only when new ideas, technology, quality and value are not available in the UK.

Ensuring staff and shareholders share in the success of the Company.

Constantly seeking to improve quality standards in all areas of the Company's operations.

Fostering good human relations with customers, staff, suppliers and the community.

Acting responsibly towards the environment in all our operations and, with our suppliers, in the manufacture of the goods we sell.

St Michael

---

63   McDonald's Restaurants Ltd   Fast food
UK

"There's nothing quite like a McDonald's"

Corporate mission 1992–2000
To be the United Kingdom's number one and favourite quick service restaurant. The company will be led by the needs of our customers and committed to the welfare and development of our staff. McDonald's will provide great tasting food, backed up by excellent operations and friendly service in a relaxed, safe and consistent restaurant environment. Our customers will be served in a caring, welcoming and professional manner. These goals will be implemented in a way which optimises the highest operational standards with efficiency and profitability.

---

64   McKinsey & Co Inc   Management
USA   consultants

McKinsey mission
To help our clients make positive, lasting, and substantial improvements in their performance and to build a great Firm that is able to attract, develop, excite, and retain exceptional people.

Guiding principles

Serving clients

- Adhere to professional standards
- Follow the top management approach
- Assist the client in implementation and capability building
- Perform consulting in a cost-effective manner

Building the firm

- Operate as one Firm
- Maintain a meritocracy
- Show a genuine concern for our people
- Foster an open and nonhierarchical working atmosphere
- Manage the Firm's resources responsibly

Being a member of the professional staff

- Demonstrate commitment to client service
- Strive continuously for superior quality
- Advance the state of the art of management
- Contribute to a spirit of partnership through teamwork and collaboration
- Profit from the freedom and assume the responsibility associated with self-governance
- Uphold the obligation to dissent

---

65   MEPC plc   Property
UK

MEPC is a major property investment company, operating in Europe, United States of America and Australia. Our worldwide portfolio is valued at £2.9 billion with 78% of the properties located in the United Kingdom. Our goal is to own and manage a diverse portfolio of commercial property investments and to concentrate on creating value for shareholders by meeting the property needs of business.

MEPC's aims

For our tenants – to provide quality buildings and an outstanding management service.

For the communities where our buildings are located – to bring lasting benefits through the refurbishment of existing properties, the design of new buildings and a commitment to progressive environmental policies.

For our shareholders – to secure long-term growth in assets per share and dividends which exceed the rate of inflation.

---

66 Merrill Lynch & Co Inc   Financial services USA

"The difference is Merrill Lynch"

Our mission is to be a client-focused, worldwide financial services organization, striving for excellence by serving the needs of individuals, corporations, governments and institutions. Our objective is to be the acknowledged leader in the value we offer our clients, the returns we offer our shareholders and the rewards we offer our employees.

Realizing our mission

In realizing our mission we will be guided by our vision of the future, a focus on our clients and markets, the need for a highly skilled and motivated organizational team, and a commitment to profitability and sound financial management.

Our vision of the future

We envision a new financial services world – one of great challenge and equally great opportunity. It will be an era of dynamic change characterized by the globalization of financial markets, instantaneous communication and intense competition. The prospect for growth in our markets is excellent, driven by ever more sophisticated and complex needs of our clients.

More than ever before, ours is becoming a business of risk management. Our ability to take prudent risk, to manage it and turn it to our clients' and Firm's advantage is fundamental to achieving our mission.

Clients and markets

Our strategies begin and end with our clients. Our progress will be measured by how well we earn the loyalty necessary for long-term client relationships. These relationships provide the foundation for the firm's success. We will win client loyalty by providing value-added products and services, differentiated by unique expertise and responsiveness.

Success will require new skills and agility to respond competitively to the rapidly changing needs of our clients. We must seek out the most talented people and the newest, most resourceful ideas. We will combine entrepreneurial perspective, technology and discipline in order to focus our resources creatively and efficiently in diverse markets worldwide.

We will build globally on our investment services base in consumer and capital markets. We will focus only on those businesses where we can achieve a dominant position and superior profitability.

Our consumer markets businesses will concentrate on serving the integrated financial services needs of the affluent and very affluent individuals, small businesses and small institutions, primarily in the United States. Our capital markets businesses will provide financing, advisory and investment services to large corporations, institutions and governments on a worldwide basis.

Organization and values

Merrill Lynch will organize its separate operations in ways that better enable us to anticipate and respond to changing client needs. Authority and accountability will be placed at levels which allow our professionals to make the best decisions on behalf of our clients and our Firm.

We are 'One Firm' with a number of separate but related operations. This enables us to leverage our resources and positions in different markets worldwide in response to specific client needs. The integrating philosophy of our diverse businesses is reflected in shared values and in our approach to managing our people, capital and corporate reputation.

As a Firm we share a powerful sense of identity. We are dedicated to the values on which this identity was built – a winning spirit and a standard of excellence in all that we do. We value integrity, leadership, the entrepreneurial spirit, and hard work. We value the individual.

At the same time, ours is an increasingly complex and competitive world, often requiring multiple perspectives and cooperation among our people. Teamwork is critical. This sharing of knowledge and skills is the common thread that binds our people together in response to specific client needs.

Financial

We are a strategically focused organization. We manage through objectives, guided by formal management systems which measure performance and promote productive use of our resources. The success or failure of our strategy will be measured by the creation of value for our stockholders.

We recognize that, in the long term, only the most efficient organizations will survive, let alone prevail, in an intensely competitive environment. We must rigorously control our costs, improve our productivity – and measure our progress in terms of profit, not volume.

We believe that the Firm's future depends on maintaining sound financial controls, a well-managed and growing capital base, and earnings stability in the face of volatile markets. This, in turn, will protect the Firm's crucial reputation for financial strength.

Merrill Lynch has a solid foundation for accomplishing this mission. The Firm's significant resources, most importantly our people, represent the critical building blocks. We have a strong market position in both consumer and capital markets worldwide and a long standing reputation for competitive spirit with the courage and understanding to manage risk. This will enable us to successfully build on Merrill Lynch's legacy of leadership in the value we offer our clients, the returns we offer our shareholders and the rewards we offer our employees.

---

67   Meyer International plc   Building materials
UK

Meyer International is the leading distributor of building materials and timber in the United Kingdom and the Netherlands.

Our main objective is to meet customer needs in the building, construction and house improvement industries with the highest possible standards of service.

Our commitment is to expand the business at home and overseas in clearly defined markets and generate increasing profit for shareholders through staff dedication and skills.

We strive both to be a good employer and to have concern for environmental and community interests wherever we operate.

---

68   Microsoft   Software
USA

"Making it all make sense"

We shall work with our customers to deliver superior products and services, making it easier for anyone to harness the power of personal computing to their best advantage.

---

69   NFC plc   Services
UK

Mission statement
NFC aims to become the world's leading logistics and trans-

port company which earns a premium return for its shareholders by supplying high quality customer focused services through a workforce which shares in the ownership of the business.

Core values

Quality is inherent in the way we run the business and in the service we provide to our customers. *Internationalism* is the essence of our ambition to become one of the world's foremost international businesses. *Employee ownership* gives us a competitive edge and benefits the company, its employees and its shareholders. *People development* means we have a commitment to invest in our employees to enable them to reach their full potential. *Social responsibilities* reflect our resolve to contribute to the communities and environments in which we operate. *Premium performance* only comes from living and working by our core values which aim to deliver the best results for all our shareholders.

---

70   Northern Electric   Electricity
UK

"The heart of the north"

Northern Electric is one of the twelve regional electricity companies of England and Wales.

We distribute and supply electricity to over 1.4 million customers in the counties of Northumberland, Tyne and Wear, Durham, Cleveland and North Yorkshire and we have a chain of more than 50 shops selling electrical appliances and audio equipment.

Our aim is to achieve high standards of service and efficiency and to operate our business in an enterprising and innovative manner, so as to create value for our shareholders, customers and employees.

---

71   Northern Foods plc   Foods
UK

Northern Foods is the United Kingdom's most broadly based fresh food manufacturer. We produce a wide range of high quality chilled foods under the 'own labels' of major retailers and leading brands including Ski, Eden Vale, Pork Farms, Bowyers and Hollands. We are also Britain's largest supplier of liquid milk to households and shops, under the Dale Farm and Express brands and retailer labels. Our grocery interests include Fox's, the leading name in premium quality biscuits.

We produce foods to the highest standards of quality and reliability and are skilled in the safe handling of short-life products. Our commitment to customer service, product freshness and innovation is supported by constant investment in new facilities and improved technology.

We will continue to grow by meeting our customers' increasing demands for consistent quality, variety and value.

The company's objective in implementing these policies is to improve the prospects of shareholders, employees and the communities in which we operate.

---

72   Ocean Group plc   Industrial services
UK

Ocean's **Purpose** is to be outstanding as an international provider of industrial and distribution services.

To achieve this we will:

- Perform all our activities to high standards of **Quality**

- Develop lasting, innovative relationships with our **Customers**

- Ensure our businesses are **Leaders** in their markets.

All this depends on our **People**. They are the key to achieving our Purpose and we are committed to developing their potential to the full.

---

73   Oxford Engineering UK

Engineering

Mission statement

The vision is simply: 'To be an Engineering Company Worthy of High Regard.'

This mission statement is to let all interested parties know what we are about and where we are going. It should help all employees to pull in the same direction. It is not just pretty words but an honest statement of intent as seen by senior management. It is not highly ambitious, over reaching or unobtainable. We do not claim that we want to be the biggest or the best. We believe that if in every aspect of the business we warrant 'high regard', then success, in both human and financial terms, will follow.

Those involved with our vision:

Customers
- Who give us their business and expect us to satisfy their needs.

Employees
- Who provide their skill and commitment and expect remuneration and appreciation.

Bankers
- Who provide us with the funds to operate the business and expect a return on their investment and for the company to operate responsibly.

Suppliers
- Who provide us with goods and services and who expect payment and understanding.

Community
- Who constitute the environment in which we live and work, within which we want to act with responsibility.

Our company values
Customers
- To behave with integrity and honesty in all aspects of our dealings with customers.

Employees
- To respect the individual and when able, to err towards more generous remuneration.
- To expect high performance standards from employees.
- To provide where possible job satisfaction, recognising that the company is 'people'.
- To train employees to make them more able for the tasks expected of them.
- Where possible to promote from within.

Suppliers
- To display integrity and to be honest in all aspects of our dealings with suppliers.

Work-place
- To maintain good and safe working conditions, above the industry norm, with an accent on cleanliness.

Company
- To remain a private limited company.

Strategy
The company's strategies are the means by which we strive to achieve our vision. The list of strategies that follow do not appear in any particular order of priority. They should be read as a coordinated and coherent whole, as a group of strategies which, taken together, will enable us to achieve our vision.

1. To operate towards the leading edge of technology and to invest sufficiently in our people and equipment to ensure a high level of competence.
2. To aim our service and goods to that sector that displays

the best current growth and financial performance, having due regard to opportunism, local and existing customers.

3. We are committed to continual Quality Improvement that emphasises the accountability of every employee to product and work-place quality.

4. We are committed to exemplary customer service, particularly with regard to 'delivery to promise' and our aim towards 'zero defect'.

5. To seek closer relationships with our customers, leading in some cases to 'Partnership Sourcing'.

6. To make it a delightful experience to be a customer of Oxford Engineering. Likewise endeavour for it to be a delightful experience to work for Oxford Engineering.

7. Continual cost reduction and efficiency improvements will be aggressively pursued by all.

8. Progressive improvement in financial performance and control of costs.

9. Profit to be re-invested in line with our policy of continual progress.

10. Every effort will be made to encourage team spirit with emphasis on employee involvement.

11. Vigorous and effective marketing of our services and products.

12. Seeking quality goods and services from our suppliers on a competitive basis while fostering long-term, mutually supportive, relationships with them.

13. Investment in training. We believe that a well-trained workforce will out-perform a company of untrained people no matter how much natural ability they may have.

---

74 J C Penney Co Inc   Retailing
USA

Mission statement: the Penney idea

1. To serve the public, as nearly as we can, to its complete satisfaction.
2. To expect for the service we render a fair remuneration and not all the profit the traffic will bear.
3. To do all in our power to pack the customer's dollar full of value, quality, and satisfaction.
4. To continue to train ourselves and our associates so that the service we give will be more and more intelligently performed.
5. To improve constantly the human factor in our business.
6. To reward men and women in our organization through participation in what the business produces.
7. To test our every policy, method, and act in this wise: 'Does it square with what is right and just?'

Adopted 1913

---

75 Philips Dictation Systems   Office equipment
Austria

"The sign of a better manager"

Mission statement
At Philips Dictation Systems we serve people and organisations around the world in their need to capture ideas, thoughts or information, and prepare these for communication and reference.

To meet these needs we will develop, produce and market products that offer improved ways of capturing and transforming the spoken word so it can be read, stored and distributed as needed.

Our aim is to be the recognised leader in this field, utilising and integrating with new technology to provide exciting innovative solutions for our customers.

Our future success will be founded on our commitment to these guiding principles and commonly shared values:

- Our Focus is Our Customer
- Our Foundation is Our People
- Our Core is Quality
- Our Challenge is Innovation
- We Will Grow Our Business
- We Will be Responsible

In adhering to these guiding principles and values, we will build a company we are proud to be associated with: proud of our ability to meet user needs, of our world leadership position, of our people and of our products.

Our Focus is Our Customer

- Our users – and their needs – will be the focal point for every decision and action we take.
- Where our dealers are our first-line customers, we will do our utmost to satisfy their needs to our mutual benefit.
- We will be more effective than our competitors in understanding, anticipating and meeting our customers' needs.

Our Foundation is Our People

- Our people and their determination form the cornerstone of our success. We would rather they try hard and fail, than not try at all.
- We believe in teamwork – our managers will build a team environment based on caring, honesty and candid communication.
- Integrity, consistency and decisiveness will be our guide. We will be fair, reliable and trustworthy.

Our Core is Quality

- We will only do what we can do properly and thoroughly.
- We will use our own know-how and experience – and Philips' resources as a whole – to deliver quality, reliability and efficacy in our products and systems.

Our Challenge is Innovation

- Innovation – in products, sales and marketing – is an integral component of our formula for growth.
- We will research and apply current and emerging technologies to ensure that our products integrate with and add benefit to our users' own communication environments.

We Will Grow Our Business

- We will continue as a dedicated organisation, with a global presence under the brand name Philips. (In USA, Philips and Norelco.)
- We will grow our global markets through user-oriented marketing, product development, sales and service initiatives.
- We will set ambitious goals and be determined in achieving results.

We Will be Responsible

- We have a duty to our parent Philips which we will carry out fully.
- We will always be considerate towards the environment and society in which we work.

---

76   Pilkington Glass Ltd   Glass
UK

"The world's leading glass company"

PGL mission statement
Our objective is to be the most profitable company in the core Flat and Safety Glass industries which we serve, and to sustain this for the benefit of our shareholders by being responsive to our markets and by creating and holding a position of cost leadership.

We will achieve these objectives by:

- An overriding commitment to the architectural and automotive markets in the UK, Europe and throughout the world.
- Sensitivity to the needs of our customers.
- Establishing cost leadership, in order to reflect our dependence on commodity products.
- Developing a quality culture in every aspect of our business and service to the customer, to win and hold a competitive edge.
- Promoting an environment in which individuals adopt calculated risk-taking as an intrinsic part of business activity.
- Ownership of our problems.
- Creating an environment for change which will enable our response to business needs, and to opportunities, to be made faster.
- Striving for the highest standards in all aspects of our business, motivated by an acute awareness of the best international practices.
- A commitment to grow demand for Basic Glass through market and technical leadership.
- Continuing to lead the world in Flat Glass manufacturing technology.
- Recognising that all of our objectives can only be achieved through the positive contribution of every individual.

Confirmed by the Pilkington Glass Board, 18th July 1990

Rodney Stansfield, Chief Executive

---

77 Procter & Gamble USA

Fast-moving consumer goods

A statement of purpose
We will provide products of superior quality and value that best fill the needs of the world's consumers.

We will achieve that purpose through an organization and a working environment which attracts the finest people; fully develops and challenges our individual talents; encourages our free and spirited collaboration to drive the business ahead; and maintains the Company's historic principles of integrity, and doing the right thing.

Through the successful pursuit of our commitment, we expect our brands to achieve leadership share and profit positions and that, as a result, our business, our people, our shareholders, and the communities in which we live and work, will prosper.

These are the principles that guide our actions as a Company and our attitudes about our employees:

- We will employ, throughout the Company, the best people we can find without regard to race or gender or any other differences unrelated to performance. We will promote on the same basis.

- We recognize the vital importance of continuing employment because of its ultimate tie with the strength and success of our business.

- We will build our organization from within. Those persons with ability and performance records will be given the opportunity to move ahead in the Company.

- We will pay our employees fairly, with careful attention to the compensation of each individual. Our benefit programs will be designed to provide our employees with adequate protection in time of need.

- We will encourage and reward individual innovation, personal initiative and leadership, and willingness to manage risk.

- We will encourage teamwork across disciplines, divisions and geography to get the most effective integration of the ideas and efforts of our people.

- We will maximize the development of individuals through training and coaching on what they are doing well and how they can do better. We will evaluate Procter & Gamble managers on their record in developing their subordinates.

- We will maintain and build our corporate tradition which is rooted in the principles of personal integrity; doing what's right for the long term; respect for the individual; and being the best in what we do.

These are the things that will enable us to achieve the category leadership that is our goal in every business in which we compete:

- We will develop a superior understanding of consumers and their needs. This is the foundation and impetus for generating the superior benefits and value consumers seek in our brands.

- We will develop strategies and plans capable of giving us the competitive advantage needed to meet our business objectives.

- We will create and deliver product and packaging on all our brands which provide a compelling advantage versus competition in bringing consumers superior benefits that best satisfy their needs. To do this we will be the world leader in the relevant science and technology.

- We will seek significant and sustainable competitive advantages in quality, cost and service in our total supply and delivery systems so as to meet our business objectives.

- We will have superior, creative marketing on all our brands. We will have enduring superior copy, and promotion programs distinguished by their creativity, effectiveness, and efficiency.

- We will develop close, mutually productive relationships with our trade customers and our suppliers. We will work with these partners in ways that are good for both of our businesses.

- We will promote a sense of urgency and a willingness to try new things. This will enable us to get better ideas working in the market ahead of competition.

- We will follow the principles of Total Quality to achieve continual improvement in everything we do. Whatever level of performance we have achieved today, we know that we can and must improve upon it tomorrow.

---

78   Reed Elsevier   Publishing
UK/Netherlands

Reed Elsevier is one of the world's largest publishing and information groups. Its activities include scientific, professional, business to business and consumer publishing. It is well established in the USA, the UK, the Netherlands and Australia and is expanding in continental Europe and Asia. It has annual sales in excess of £2.5 billion and 25,000 employees.

Reed Elsevier's strategy is to concentrate on publishing and information through international businesses with market-leading positions in large or growing markets. Its style is decentralised, enabling each operating company to stay close to its market-place while operating within strict strategic and financial controls.

The group's financial objective is to achieve an increase in shareholder value through organic development and, using its strong cash flow, by making appropriate acquisitions.

Reed Elsevier is owned equally by the UK company, Reed International plc and the Dutch company, Elsevier NV. The businesses merged on 1 January 1993 and are now managed on a unified basis. Both companies are listed on the London and Amsterdam stock exchanges and the returns to their shareholders are equalised in terms of dividend and capital rights.

---

79   Reuters Holdings plc   Information services UK

"Making the best information work harder"

Reuters informs the world instantly by the latest electronic means. We help our customers to analyse the facts and trade on them.

We dedicate the bulk of our resources to serving banks, brokers and other organisations involved in financial markets. Inseparable from this is the company's other main activity – the supply of news services to the world's media.

Our customers watch news and prices on some 200,000 computer screens linked to a Reuters communications network spanning more than 130 countries. We supply data-management products which enable customers to compare information from a variety of sources in displays which they create themselves. They analyse trends based on our price histories and software programs. They use Reuter terminals to negotiate with their chosen counter-parties. Alternatively, our computers will match them with a buyer or seller automatically.

Reuters customers demand speed and accuracy above all else. In fast-moving markets, they require quick access to the latest information, backed by high quality service and a commitment to rapid technical innovation. Reuters has a 140-year tradition of accuracy, shared by our 10,000 employees. This tradition is rooted in our independence, which we jealously guard. It is outlined in the principles of our Trust, preventing the company from falling under the influence of any interest group.

---

80 Rockwell International USA

Aerospace, electronics, automotive, graphics

"Where science gets down to business"

The Rockwell credo

What we believe

We believe maximizing the satisfaction of our customers is our most important concern as a means of warranting their continued loyalty.

We believe in providing superior value to customers through high-quality, technologically advanced, fairly priced products and customer service, designed to meet customer needs better than all alternatives.

We believe Rockwell people are our most important assets, making the critical difference in how well Rockwell performs; and, through their work and effort, separating Rockwell from all competitors.

We believe we have an obligation for the well-being of the communities in which we live and work.

We believe excellence is the standard for all we do, achieved by encouraging and nourishing:

- Respect for the individual
- Honest, open communication
- Individual development and satisfaction
- A sense of ownership and responsibility for Rockwell's success
- Participation, cooperation and teamwork
- Creativity, innovation and initiative
- Prudent risk-taking
- Recognition and rewards for achievement

We believe success is realized by:

- Achieving leadership in the markets we serve
- Focusing our resources and energy on global markets

where our technology, knowledge, capabilities and understanding of customers combine to provide the opportunity for leadership

- Maintaining the highest standards of ethics and integrity in every action we take, in everything we do

We believe the ultimate measure of our success is the ability to provide a superior value to our shareowners, balancing near-term and long-term objectives to achieve both competitive return on investment and consistent increased market value.

---

81   The Royal Bank of Scotland Group plc
UK   Bank

"Where people matter"

Corporate statement
The Royal Bank of Scotland Group, headquartered in Edinburgh, provides high quality, competitively priced banking, insurance and related financial services.

Our core market is the United Kingdom. We are active in Europe to serve and develop our UK commercial banking customer base, and in the north-east USA to diversify our earnings.

We aim to be recognised as the best financial institution in the United Kingdom. In striving towards that aim we are mindful of our responsibilities to:

- *Shareholders*, who entrust us with stewardship of our capital;
- *Customers*, who confide management of their affairs to us;
- *Employees*, who commit their careers to us; and
- The *Communities* in which we operate.

Achieving our aim while successfully balancing these responsibilities is the primary challenge. We believe that we can best respond to this challenge by remaining independent.

---

82   Royal Dutch/Shell Group of Companies   Oil
The Netherlands/UK

"You can be sure of Shell"

Introduction

This reaffirms the general business principles on which the conduct of the affairs of the Royal Dutch/Shell Group of Companies is predicated. They apply equally to corporate decision-making as to the individual behaviour expected of employees in conducting Shell business. They are commended to staff of the Service Companies in London and The Hague as well as to management of Operating Companies.

The Group is typified by decentralized, highly diversified and widespread operations, with which operating companies are given freedom of action. However, the upholding of the Shell reputation is a common bond which can be maintained only by honesty and integrity in all activities. A single failure, whether it be wilful or due to misplaced zeal, or short-term expendiency, can have very serious effects on the Group as a whole.

These principles have served Shell companies well for many years and will continue to do so in the future. The statement is available for wide distribution within the Royal Dutch/Shell Group and merits periodic re-reading. It may be exhibited externally as required.

Statement of general business principles

1. Objectives
The objectives of Shell companies are to engage efficiently, responsibly and profitably in the oil, gas, chemicals, coal, metals and other selected business, and to play an active role in the search for and development of other sources of energy. Shell companies seek a high standard of performance and aim to maintain a long-term position in their respective competitive environments.

2. *Responsibilities*
Four areas of responsibility are recognized:

(a) To shareholders
To protect shareholders' investment and provide an acceptable return.

(b) To employees
To provide all employees with good and safe conditions of work, good and competitive terms and conditions of service; to promote the development and best use of human talent and equal-opportunity employment; and to encourage the involvement of employees in the planning and direction of their work, recognizing that success depends on the full contribution of all employees.

(c) To customers
To develop and provide products and services which offer value in terms of price and quality, supported by the requisite technological and commercial expertise. There is no guaranteed future: Shell companies depend on winning and maintaining customers' support.

(d) To society
To conduct business as responsible corporate members of society, observing applicable laws of the countries in which they operate giving due regard to safety and environmental standards and societal aspirations.

These four areas of responsibility are seen as inseparable. Therefore, it is the duty of management continuously to assess the priorities and discharge its responsibilities as best it can on the basis of that assessment.

3. *Economic principles*
Profitability is essential to discharging these responsibilities and staying in business. It is a measure both of efficiency and of the ultimate value that people place on Shell products and services. It is essential to the proper allocation of corporate resources and necessary to support the continuing invest-

ment required to develop and produce future energy supplies to meet consumer needs. Without profits and a strong financial foundation, it would not be possible to fulfil the responsibilities outlined above.

Shell companies work in a wide variety of social, political and economic environments over the nature of which they have little influence, but in general they believe that the interests of the community can be served most efficiently by a market economy.

Criteria for investment decisions are essentially economic but also take into account social and environmental considerations and an appraisal of the security of the investment.

4. Voluntary codes of conduct

Policies of Shell companies are consistent with the two existing internationally agreed voluntary codes of conduct for multinational enterprises, namely the OECD Declaration and Guidelines for International Investment and Multinational Enterprises and the ILO Tripartite Declaration of Principles.

5. Business integrity

Shell companies insist on honesty and integrity in all aspects of their business. All employees are required to avoid conflicts of interest between their private financial activities and their part in the conduct of company business. The offer, payment, soliciting and acceptance of bribes in any form are unacceptable practices. All transactions on behalf of a Shell company must be appropriately described in the accounts of the company in accordance with established procedures and be subject to audit.

6. Political activities

(a) Companies

Shell companies endeavour always to act commercially, operating within existing national laws in a socially responsible manner, abstaining from participation in party politics. It is, however, their legitimate right and responsibility to speak out on matters that affect the interests of employees, customers and shareholders, and on matters of general interest, where they have a contribution to make that is based on particular knowledge.

(b) Political payments

As a policy, Shell companies do not make payments to political parties, organizations or their representatives.

(c) Employees

Where employees, in their capacity as citizens, wish to engage in activities in their community, including standing for election to public office, favourable consideration is given to their being enabled to do so where this is appropriate in the light of local circumstances.

7. *Environment*

It is the policy of Shell companies to conduct their activities in such a way as to take foremost account of the health and safety of their employees and of other persons, and to give proper regard to the conservation of the environment. In implementing this policy, Shell companies not only comply with the requirements of the relevant legislation but promote in an appropriate manner measures for the protection of health, safety and the environment for all who may be affected directly or indirectly in their activities.

Such measures pertain to safety of operations carried out by employees and contractors; product safety; prevention of air, water and soil pollution; and precautions to minimise damage from such accidents as may nevertheless occur.

8. *The community*

The most important contribution that companies can make to the social and material progress of the countries in which they operate is in performing their basic activities as efficiently as possible. In addition, the need is recognized to take a constructive interest in societal matters which may not be directly related to the business. Opportunities for involvement – for example through community, educational or donations programmes – will vary depending upon the size of the company concerned, the nature of the local society, and the scope for useful private initiatives.

9. Information

The importance of the activities in which Shell companies are engaged and their impact on national economies and individuals are well recognized. Full relevant information about these activities is therefore provided to legitimately interested parties, both national and international, subject to any overriding consideration of confidentiality proper to the protection of the business and the interests of third parties.

10. Application

The reputation of the Royal Dutch/Shell Group of Companies depends on the existence and knowledge of clearly understood principles and responsibilities and on their observance in day-to-day practice in widely different environments. Individual operating companies may elaborate their own statements to meet national situations, but this Statement of General Business Principles serves as the basis on which companies of the Royal Dutch/Shell Group, in their operations, pursue the highest standards of behaviour.

Group companies are involved in many joint ventures. Shell companies participating in many joint ventures will promote the application of these principles and will take into account their ability to do so in deciding whether to participate in any joint venture.

---

83 RTZ Corporation plc Mining
UK

"Bringing out the best in the world"

RTZ, based in Britain, is a world leader in the international mining industry. The company's unique product and geographical diversity provides a firm foundation from which to manage both short-term change and profitable growth for its shareholders into the next century.

RTZ's strategy is to concentrate on the development of large, high quality mineral deposits. Its mining interests include: copper, gold, iron ore, aluminium, lead, zinc and silver in metals; coal and uranium in energy; and borax, titanium dioxide feedstock, talc, diamonds and zircon in other minerals. They are located predominantly in North America and Australasia as well as in Europe, Southern Africa and South America. Products are sold worldwide, with a substantial proportion to the high growth Pacific Rim. In addition, RTZ has substantial UK and North American industrial businesses supplying products and services to the construction and engineering industries.

By the very nature of mining, RTZ has a long-term perspective, both in building the wealth of its shareholders and in contributing to society. Developing and sustaining an international mining business of this magnitude has meant building a management team with a special approach. This requires a commitment to devolving operational decision-making within a disciplined, strategic framework, to enhancing the capabilities of its employees, and to transferring skills around the world.

RTZ's aim is to act responsibly as the steward of the resources in its charge, working for the well being of the communities and countries where they are found, adopting best contemporary practice in environmental matters, and seeking health and safety performance second to none in mining.

In short, RTZ accepts and welcomes the responsibilities which accompany leadership in supplying the essential natural resources which are major contributors to economic and social prosperity.

---

84 Russell Reynolds Associates UK

Executive search

Our mission is to provide a select group of clients worldwide with executive search consulting of the highest quality. We seek to build long-term relationships by providing our clients with superior value and service, through a commitment to international teamwork, disciplined knowledge of markets and industries, and integrity in all we do.

---

85   Safeway Stores plc   Food retailing
UK

"Where good ideas come naturally"

We are committed to creating an enduring food retail business. We aim to be a leader in our industry . . .

Food expertise and customer service are key to our reputation as a quality, caring company. Profit is the measure of our success. It provides a fair return to our shareholders and secures our long-term future.

We serve our customers . . .
We take pride in imaginatively anticipating and responding to the national, regional and local needs of our customers. We will provide them with a significantly wider choice of high quality products and excellent value, in an attractive and convenient shopping environment.

We value our people . . .
We will create an atmosphere in which our people can develop their talents and contribute as part of an energetic and enthusiastic team. We will invest in recruitment and training. We will reward them for achievement through the resourceful application of knowledge and skills.

We work in partnership with our suppliers . . .
We acknowledge common interest with our suppliers in meeting customer needs. While we will be exacting customers, we will be fair in all our dealings. We aim to develop long-term relationships of mutual respect and understanding with our suppliers and trading partners.

We participate in our communities . . .
We will build a reputation for making a positive and responsible contribution to the environment and to the lives of the communities in which we live and work. We will be recognised as good neighbours.

We support our industry . . .
We are proud of the food industry in which we are involved. We shall continue to work with our colleagues to achieve improved efficiency, higher standards of product safety and better employment practices. We will communicate with government and local authorities in both the UK and Europe to ensure our industry is properly represented.

We reward our shareholders . . .
We will effectively manage our resources so as to ensure a worthwhile return on our assets and to provide increasing returns to our shareholders.

---

86   J Sainsbury plc UK   Food retailing

"Good food costs less at Sainsbury's"

Mission statement: company objectives
To discharge the responsibility as leaders in our trade by acting with complete integrity, by carrying out our work to the highest standards, and by contributing to the public good and to the quality of life in the community.

To provide unrivalled value to our customers in the quality of the goods we sell, in the competitiveness of our prices and the range of choice we offer.

In our stores, to achieve the highest standards of cleanliness and hygiene, efficiency of operation, convenience and customer service, and thereby create as attractive and friendly a shopping environment as possible.

To offer our staff outstanding opportunities in terms of personal career development and in remuneration relative to other companies in the same market, practising always a concern for the welfare of every individual.

To generate sufficient profit to finance continual improvement and growth of the business whilst providing our shareholders with an excellent return on their investment.

---

87   Scottish Power   Electricity
UK

The Scottish Power mission statement
To be recognised as a highly rated utility-based company trading in electricity, other utility and related markets providing excellent quality and service to customers and above average total returns to investors.

88   The Scout Association   Association
UK

"Be prepared"

The aim of the Scout Association is to promote the development of young people in achieving their full physical, intellectual, social and spiritual potentials, as individuals, as responsible citizens and as members of their local, national and international communities.

89   Sedgwick Group plc   Financial services
UK

Sedgwick provides risk consultancy, insurance broking, employee benefits consultancy and financial services from more than 230 locations in 58 countries.

Sedgwick's goal is to win with quality wherever the group operates, through the expertise of its staff, by its commitment to providing an ever-increasing level of service for its clients, by improving shareholder value and through its relationship as a good citizen of the communities of which it is a part.

90   Shandwick plc   Public relations
UK

Mission statement
We strive to be the most progressive public relations group
in the world by providing a high quality and disciplined
service, achieving a measurable difference for clients,
encouraging and rewarding the professional excellence of
our people and ensuring long-term prosperity for our shareholders.

---

91   WH Smith Group plc   Retailing
UK

"There's more to discover at WH Smith"

Group vision
Our goal is to offer a range of products and a quality of service
which meet our customers' needs more effectively than any
of our competitors.

We want all who work for the Group to contribute as
much as they can to its success. We will develop a climate
which emphasises directness, openness to new ideas, personal accountability and the recognition of individual and
team achievement.

By attaining our goal, we will achieve a consistent and
competitive growth in our profits and earnings for the benefit
of our shareholders, our staff and the community.

Group strategy statement
Our goal is to be recognised as the leading company in each
of our markets and to maintain standards of excellence in
everything we do that will distinguish us from our competitors.

Our strategy is to focus on businesses in which our core
skills and experience in retailing and distribution can be
brought to bear. Each business will aim to be a leader in its
own area, enjoying a sufficient market share to achieve the

scale benefits available to market leaders. The Group will add value to its businesses by fostering and guiding their strategies, by facilitating the development and sharing of skills between businesses, and by coordinating the strategies of different businesses that are addressing overlapping markets.

The Group will concentrate on the retailing and distribution of books, news, stationery, recorded music, video and related products: these are businesses that can draw on the Group's knowledge and skills, in particular in the management and control of multiple line item retailing and distribution. The Group will build on the strong positions it already enjoys in these businesses in the UK, and will seek to develop similar strengths in the USA and Europe.

Group purpose and role
The main purpose of the WH Smith Group is to achieve a consistent growth in profits and earnings for the benefit of our shareholders, our staff and the community. We want to be regarded as a leading company, judged by the high standard of both our achievement and our performance.

The Group's businesses sell books, newspapers and magazines, stationery products, recorded music and video. In each of these markets we aim to be a leader and to spread geographically in Britain, Europe and North America.

The WH Smith Group serves various communities and for each we should aim for the highest standards.

For our customers we should aim to offer an exceptional range of products combining basic needs, quality, value for money and originality. We should aim always to give excellent service, so that we are considered to be the best in our field.

For our staff we should aim to give a good career at whatever level. We must recruit the best people for the job. We must aim to reward people well, train and develop them for their job and for promotion, and provide good conditions for work. We must communicate and consult with them, set high standards, always be fair and treat every individual with a sense of dignity. We want to make work enjoyable and rewarding.

For our shareholders we should provide a satisfactory

growth in the value of the Company and in the income they get from it. We should keep them well informed and encourage them to think as owners.

For our suppliers we will aim to forge a lasting link, developing a relationship from which both sides will prosper. We should always treat our suppliers fairly and expect high standards from them in return.

To the community we will contribute as good citizens. We will be aware of the effect of our actions on the environment and follow a code of good practice. We will contribute through our support of the arts and education and through donations to charitable activities. We will encourage our staff to be involved in community affairs.

In all our activities we should act with integrity, consideration and good humour. Our motto should be 'Only the best will do'.

Group style of leadership

The WH Smith Group should be an organisation in which:

1. Those who work for it are proud of it and feel responsible for its success.
2. All staff have an opportunity to contribute, learn and grow, with progress based on merit and performance.
3. All staff are respected, treated fairly, listened to and involved.
4. Staff achieve real satisfaction from their accomplishments and business friendships and enjoy their place of work.
5. A style of leadership is developed which:

    (a) Exemplifies directness, openness to ideas, commitment to the success of others, a willingness to accept personal accountability and the strong development of teamwork and trust. Differing views will be sought, valued and honestly encouraged, not suppressed.

    (b) Follows clear and well-understood decision-making processes, which take account of all relevant views and information.

    (c) Is clear about Group, team and individual performance goals. People must have a clear understanding of their responsibilities and their performance targets.

(d) Values staff throughout the organisation, makes full use of the skills and abilities of people, and provides training and development to best-practice standards in all areas.

(e) Provides recognition to individuals and teams who contribute to our success. Recognition must be given to all who contribute, ie those who create and innovate, as well as those who routinely support the day-to-day business. People must be given an honest appraisal of their performance and career prospects.

(f) Practises by example high standards of ethical behaviour. We need to provide clarity in our expectations and enforce standards across the Group.

(g) Increases the authority and responsibility of those closest to our products and our customers. By actively pushing responsibility, trust and recognition throughout the organisation, we can release and benefit from the full capabilities of our people.

All this means building on the foundation we have inherited and reaffirming the best of our Group's traditions, closing any gaps which may exist between principles and practices and embracing emerging values that reflect best corporate practice.

---

92 Sun Life Assurance Society plc   Insurance UK

Sun *Life*
Sun Life aims to be the leading life assurance, pensions and investment company in all our chosen market sectors. We will meet our customers' needs for protection, security and investment growth and will seek to achieve total customer satisfaction through continuous improvement of our products, performance and service.

Sun *Service*

We will be **distinctive** by understanding and meeting our customers' needs in three areas:

Superior solutions
- Using technical and financial expertise to create outstanding products and services.

Superior service
- Delivering a fast, friendly and fault-free service, second to none in the industry.

Superior satisfaction
- Delivering consistently superior investment performance and providing efficient administration at below industry average cost.

Sun *Spirit*

We will deliver this commitment to industry excellence by:

- Putting the customer first at all times.
- Taking individual responsibility to satisfy customer needs.
- Maximising opportunities for self-development.
- Creating an environment of professionalism, integrity and fun.
- Valuing teamwork as the means to attain our objectives.
- Seeking continuous improvement in all our operations.
- Taking pride in Sun Life.

Sun *Spirit*   Sun *Service*   Sun *Life*

---

93   Tesco plc   Food retailing
UK

"The quest for quality continues"

Tesco is one of Britain's leading food retailers with 412 stores throughout England, Scotland and Wales, and serves more than 9 million customers every week.
Tesco is committed to:

- Offering customers the best value for money, and the most competitive prices, of any national superstore chain.
- Meeting the needs of customers by constantly seeking, and acting on, their opinions regarding product quality, choice, innovation, store facilities and service.
- Providing shareholders with outstanding returns on their investment.
- Improving profitability through investment in efficient stores and distribution depots, in productivity improvements and in new technology.
- Developing the talents of its people through sound management and training practices, while rewarding them fairly with equal opportunities for all.
- Working closely with suppliers to build long-term business relationships based on strict quality and price criteria.
- Participating in the formulation of national food industry policies on key issues such as health, nutrition, hygiene, safety and animal welfare.
- Supporting the well-being of the community and the protection of the environment.

---

94   Tomkins plc   Industrial management
UK

Tomkins is an industrial management company dedicated to the revitalisation of underdeveloped businesses and their sustained growth.

This is achieved by selective acquisition from a diverse range of low-risk technology companies with unrealised potential.

Acquired companies are revitalised as autonomous businesses through the injection of management expertise, capital for development and the application of tight financial disciplines.

Tomkins has three key objectives:

- To generate above average growth in earnings per share.
- To maintain the progressive dividend policy.
- To be broadly based by spreading shareholders' risk over a range of products, customers, markets, cycles and countries.

---

95   Toshiba   Electronics
Japan

"In touch with tomorrow"

Basic commitment of the Toshiba Group
We, the Toshiba Group companies, based on our total commitment to people and to the future, are determined to help create a higher quality of life for all people, and to do our part to help ensure that progress continues within the world community.

Commitment to people
We endeavor to serve the needs of all people, especially our customers, shareholders, and employees, by implementing forward-looking corporate strategies while carrying out responsible and responsive business activities. As good corporate citizens, we actively contribute to further the goals of society.

Commitment to the future
By continually developing innovative technologies centering on the fields of Electronics and Energy, we strive to create

products and services that enhance human life and which lead to a thriving, healthy society. We constantly seek new approaches that help realize the goals of the world community, including ways to improve the global environment.

Committed to People,
Committed to the Future. Toshiba.

---

96   Toyota Motor Corporation   Cars
Japan

"The car in front is a Toyota"

Guiding principles

1. Be a company of the world.
2. Serve the greater good of people everywhere by devoting careful attention to safety and to the environment.
3. Assert leadership in technology and in customer satisfaction.
4. Become a contributing member of the community in every nation.
5. Foster a corporate culture that honors individuality while promoting teamwork.
6. Pursue continuing growth through efficient, global management.
7. Build lasting relationships with business partners around the world.

1. Be a company of the world
Observe internationally accepted standards of corporate ethics.

- Conduct business in a manner consistent with international concepts of fairness and openness.
- Solicit opinions and advice about pertinent issues from

authoritative third parties, and take their views into consideration in framing corporate policy.

Implement personnel policy that reflects the international scope of the company's operations.

- Foster managers in every nation who understand and implement the tenets of Toyota philosophy, and provide them with meaningful opportunities for advancement, including career paths that lead to positions at corporate headquarters in Japan.
- Implement systematic programs to ensure that executives dispatched to overseas operations adopt an international perspective and a sense of involvement in the local community.

2. Serve the greater good of people everywhere by devoting careful attention to safety and to the environment
Assign top priority to safety and the environment in products and in operations.
Develop applied technology and basic technology to heighten safety and to minimize environmental impact.
Find ways – such as setting up new enterprises – to share the benefits of original advances in safety and environmental technologies.

3. Assert leadership in technology and in customer satisfaction
Provide people around the world with appealing products and services that are well matched to their needs and that fulfill reasonable expectations in regard to quality and price.

- Develop and maintain a full line of vehicles that addresses needs and circumstances in every nation.
- Develop new kinds of products that serve evolving needs for mobility.

Build and maintain a world-class team of engineers.

- Seek leadership in production technology – as well as in product technology – and also in peripheral technologies.

4. Become a contributing member of the community in every nation
Handle as much work as possible locally in every market.

- Provide operations in principal markets with capabilities for handling the entire sequence from product development through production to marketing and after-sales service.
- Equip operations in every nation with state-of-the-art technology, and provide the necessary training to develop a productive, world-class workplace.
- Manage operations in each nation in ways that maximize opportunities for employment and advancement and that promote the cultural values of the local community.

Distribute management functions globally.

- Invest local management in every region with sufficient authority to manage their operations in ways that accommodate local circumstances and values.
- Establish a clear division of labor in management between overseas operations and headquarters in Japan.

Support and upgrade local management functions overseas with an eye to making local operations individually accountable for profitability.

5. Foster a corporate culture that honors individuality while promoting teamwork
Generate synergistic gains in productivity through a dynamic fusion of individual creativity and group teamwork.

- Combine the virtues of Japanese-style teamwork with the creativity of Western-style individualism.
- Evaluate employees with objective measures of ability and performance.

Strive to heighten the appeal of careers in the automotive industry and in manufacturing in general.

- Develop new production systems and modes of work in response to changing values and lifestyles.
- Lead an industrywide effort – encompassing other automakers and suppliers – to enhance working conditions.

6. Pursue continuing growth through efficient, global management

Consider net global efficiency in distributing and using resources.

Maximize profitability and growth potential through unceasing efforts to reduce costs and raise productivity.

7. Build lasting relationships with business partners around the world

Stand ready and eager to do business with any supplier in any nation who offers products of superior quality and performance at competitive prices.

- Cultivate business relationships with an eye to mutual benefit over the long term.
- Infuse business relationships with unflagging, mutual efforts to achieve continuing advances in technology, productivity and quality.
- Take concrete measures to be readily accessible to suppliers and potential suppliers worldwide.

---

97   Virgin Atlantic Airways Ltd   Airline
UK

"The businessperson's favourite airline"

As the UK's second long-haul carrier, to build an intercontinental network concentrating on those routes with a substantial established market and clear indication of growth potential, by offering the highest possible service at lowest possible cost.

---

98 Wellcome plc UK   Pharmaceuticals

Mission

Wellcome is an international pharmaceutical company dedicated to the discovery and marketing of products that promote human health and the quality of life.

We aim to achieve superior growth in market share, earnings per share and shareholder value to the benefit of customers, employees, shareholders and the community at large.

Operating philosophy

Our operating philosophy is to:

- Meet customer needs by discovery, acquisition, development, manufacture and marketing of high quality products in a cost-effective and timely way.
- Attract and motivate personnel with the ability and commitment to excel.
- Recognise and respect individual contribution, provide and promote opportunities for personal growth and foster teamwork.
- Conduct our business ethically, with honesty and integrity.
- Work responsibly with the communities and within the environments in which we operate.

By following these principles we will build on our tradition of leadership and innovation to ensure our future success.

---

99 Whitbread plc   **Brewer**
UK

Whitbread is a major UK company with annual sales in excess of £2.5 billion. Our business has been built on strong and popular brands in pubs, restaurants, shops and beer and on our ability to manage them successfully.

We have created a distinctive and contemporary place to work. Our people are encouraged to use their imagination and foresight to anticipate customers' real needs.

We work harder than our competitors to provide better service to our customers. We believe that the best way to grow our business is to achieve standards which consistently exceed customers' expectations.

---

100 Woldingham School   **Education**
UK

Goals and criteria of Sacred Heart Education

1. Faith
2. Social justice
3. Community
4. Scholarship and intellectual values
5. Personal responsibility and growth

1. Faith
Faith which allows us to live responsibly in today's world.

Criterion 1 School life should show our Faith in practice. We should develop concrete ways by which Faith can be demonstrated in school – reflection and prayer being only two of many examples.

Criterion 2 By recognising the love of Christ, the total educational experience aims to give life perspective, meaning and hope.

Criterion 3 The Religious Studies programme probes the relationship of God to man and the world.

Criterion 4 The school encourages an atmosphere of freedom, openness and enquiry, in which all girls can develop by questioning/accepting their faith.

Criterion 5 The school encourages students to make decisions in the light of Christian principles.

Criterion 6 The school recognises and respects the beliefs of other denominations and religions, presenting itself as a Catholic institution within the ecumenical tradition of the Church.

How would we recognise our success in meeting these criteria?

- There is real involvement in the life of the church; prayer and discussion groups are well supported.
- Girls are aware of the disadvantaged in society and instinctively respond in a practical, caring way to those less fortunate than themselves.
- Students appreciate that there is more to life than academic success and recognise other qualities in each other.
- Religious Education at Woldingham is seen to relate to real life and to other areas of the curriculum (ie it is not seen in isolation).
- Students are open with each other and with staff; they do not lie or cheat and are responsible in the way they treat anyone who may fall short of ideals set.
- A spirit of enquiry exists to which there is an honest response.
- Students are aware of the formidable moral dilemmas which they will encounter in life and have the knowledge and will face these as Christians.
- Students are aware of the doubts, problems and difficulties associated with any religion. They are open to the views of others, but find strength in their own Faith and Church.

2. Social justice
A social awareness which impels to action.

Criterion 1 Students are involved in, and have knowledge of, communities less affluent than Woldingham, and realise that social injustice is widespread in the world.

Criterion 2 Being informed about world situations and aware of the ramifications, students are prepared to act in whatever way they can, recognising the need to give and share as well as to receive.

Criterion 3 Students take responsibility for their own actions; meet their commitments; and perceive the positive aspects of failure.

How would we recognise our success in meeting these criteria?

- Structures exist to promote discussion and understanding of world problems.
- Students make an effort to appreciate the problems of underprivileged and disadvantaged groups in their own countries as well as overseas.
- Students support charitable organisations generously and are prepared to give time as well as money when occasion demands.
- Existing structures within the school encourage students to become more independent and self-disciplined.

3. Community
The building of a Community prepared to look outside itself, where the emphasis is on sharing, friendship and care as reflections of our relationship with God, as we live out Christian values.

Criterion 1 Members of the school are committed to Christian values.

Criterion 2 Each individual is valued and supported in his/her individualism: the diversities of religion, race and culture are accepted.

Criterion 3 Communication is such that the school community encourages mutual trust, sharing and self-respect, allowing no place for isolation and loneliness.

Criterion 4 Communal worship is seen as a means of strengthening the bonds which hold the community together.

How would we recognise our success in meeting these criteria?

- There is active participation in the liturgical life of the school.
- The liturgy reflects a developing sense of community awareness and concern.
- There is a high level of care for each other as individuals and as members of a community.
- Students with different cultural backgrounds are fully integrated within the school community.
- The school is involved in the wider community outside the school.

4. Scholarship and intellectual values
A deep respect for scholarship and intellectual values.

Criterion 1 Enjoyment of learning is encouraged.

Criterion 2 Academic achievement is in keeping with each student's potential.

Criterion 3 There is awareness of a variety of learning and teaching styles, particularly the development of independent learning and the exchange of ideas.

Criterion 4 The curriculum implies commitment to the development of aesthetic, creative, linguistic, mathematical and scientific skills.

Criterion 5 Students are educated to make decisions for themselves.

How would we recognise our success in meeting these criteria?

- The students are lively and questioning.
- The curriculum gives students a knowledge of the world around them and helps them to have a coherent mental picture of the paths through the natural and man-made world.
- Students are learning to become more independent of the teacher and aware that education is a continuing process.
- The school environment encourages serious study and allows for individual differences and needs.

5. Personal responsibility and growth
Personal growth in an atmosphere of wise freedom.

Criterion 1 Students are encouraged to value themselves and others, recognising strengths as well as weaknesses.

Criterion 2 There are opportunities for students to widen their horizons and experience leadership.

Criterion 3 Students are confident and able to face change with equanimity.

Criterion 4 Students are encouraged to develop awareness of the environment and a social conscience which will urge them to make a positive contribution to the society in which they live.

Criterion 5 Achievement in many different fields is valued (not only academic success).

How would we recognise our success in meeting these criteria?

- Students value themselves and each other.
- The students are well motivated and use their free time effectively.
- The reward and punishment system is consistent with the Goal. It does not over-emphasise nor does it discourage risk-taking.
- Leadership training is both an explicit and implicit feature of the curriculum.

- Students are able to grow through their failure and recognise that failure is not terminal.
- Achievement in all areas is praised and rewarded.
- There is a balanced curriculum which fosters development of all aspects of the student's personality.

---

101 Young & Rubicam   Advertising
USA

The challenge to our clients . . .
Our clients' most important challenge is to enhance the unique value of their brands in an increasingly hostile, complex and competitive marketplace – a 'brand' being the differentiating promise that bonds a client's products, services or organization to its customers, stakeholders and other key constituencies.

Our promise . . .
We promise to be our clients' most valued business partners in building, leveraging, protecting and managing their brand assets, both product and corporate, through bold, innovative and measurable marketing and communications ideas.

Our success will be reflected in our ability to build strong revenues and achieve incrementally profitable growth, based on sharing with our clients the responsibility for driving their sales today in ways that also strengthen their brands tomorrow.

Fulfilling our promise means being the recognized leader at creating powerful communications and making unparalleled contributions to enhancing the total brand experience.

- Our ideas must be based on superior understanding and involvement with our clients, their customers and other constituents and a total commitment to leading-edge research that ensures we and our clients consistently lead – never follow – into the future.
- Our work must be flawless in execution, based on rigorous

thinking done in partnership with our clients and reflective of the highest possible standards of quality and productivity.

- Our people must be the most creative and best qualified professionals supported by a firm commitment to training, development, recognition and the rewards of employee ownership.

- Our professionals must be able and empowered to marshal our leading communications disciplines, strong global networks and external resources in common purpose – regardless of discipline or geography – to distinguish us, totally, from our competitors.

Timothy R V Foster – Mission Statement

I am a creative thinker, communicator, enabler, organiser, innovator and motivator, a coach.

The evidence

As a creative thinker, I generate a wide variety of ideas on a wide variety of subjects. Give me the subject and the needs and I will come up with strategies and solutions.

As a communicator, I have written 16 books so far, created over 25 videos, and written countless speeches and articles. I specialise in explaining complex and abstract subjects to people with short attention spans.

As an enabler, I get an enormous kick out of providing people with the tools for their success. I have an innate enthusiasm to make things happen that transfers to those involved. I develop and write sales-idea newsletters and seminars for a wide variety of people in business. My quarterly newsletter for Burson-Marsteller Europe, *Euronotes*, has now been copied by B-M in their other regions.

As an organiser, I help to plan and execute Burson-Marsteller's annual Burson Academy, in which their top European managers gather for an intensive four-day programme concentrating on a variety of topics. The programme helped B-M to win the *PR Week* award for excellence in in-house training in 1991, as well as B-M's own Value Added Award. In 1975, I planned and executed National Investment Seminar Week for Merrill Lynch in the USA (where I was director of advertising and sales promotion), in which every office (over 400 of them) put on an investment seminar during one week, focusing the company and the investing public on what they should be doing with their money in tough times. Merrill Lynch opened 50,000 new accounts as a result of this. The programme won the Silver Anvil Award for excellence in marketing from the Public Relations Society of America. At this time I also started the Merrill Lynch Video Network, one of the first in-house corporate TV networks. At ML president Roger Birk's suggestion, because of its style, my business plan for this was then used as a model for other business plans within the Merrill Lynch organisation.

As an innovator, I have taken the broad content of my recent books and developed a unique sponsored daily radio programme, *A Way A Day To Make It Pay*, which will start airing later in 1993. This provides daily motivational guidance to the self-employed and small business people on being more effective at what they do. Separately, I created a business that monitors and checks advertising slogans for advertising agencies and clients, called *Foster's Database of Slogos*. This was brought to life each week for a year as a quiz in *Marketing* called *Name That Brand*.

As a motivator, I target my books and other works at people who need to be shown the path to their own success. I demonstrate what can be done by the application of specific techniques or thought processes.

As a coach, I thrive on passing on knowledge and inspiration to people who have a desire to succeed. As a flying instructor I have taught people to fly. As an author and broadcaster I convey information to people in original, interesting and actionable ways. As a parent I delight in developing the creativity and communication skills of my children.

My goal
To be highly valued and in demand by those who need me.

I will do this by becoming fully recognised as an essential information and motivational resource by people who seek to better themselves in all walks of life.

My values

- I seek to deliver beyond expectations.
- I keep my commitments.
- I seek a serene, warm and nurturing family life, in pleasant and comfortable surroundings.
- The positive upbringing and education of my children is paramount.
- Honesty and the Golden Rule will be served at all times.

Category Index

Accounting	Coopers & Lybrand
Advertising	Young & Rubicam
Aerospace	Rockwell International
Airline	British Airways plc
	British Midland
	Virgin Atlantic Airways Ltd
Airports	BAA plc
Association	Automobile Association
	Factors Chain International
	Girl Guides Association
	Scout Association, The
Automotive	Dana Corporation
Bank	Lloyds Bank plc
	Royal Bank of Scotland
	Group plc, The
Brewer	Bass plc
	Whitbread plc
Building materials	Meyer International plc
Car rental	Hertz (UK) Ltd
Cars	Ford Motor Company Ltd
	Honda Motor Company
	Jaguar Cars Ltd
	Toyota Motor Corporation
Chemicals	Du Pont
	Imperial Chemical Industries plc
Computers	Apple Computer
	IBM UK Ltd

CATEGORY INDEX

Industrial	BBA Group plc
	Elswick plc
Industrial management	Tomkins plc
Information	Reuters Holdings plc
Insurance	Sedgwick Group plc
	Sun Life Assurance Society plc
Library	British Library, The
Management consulting	Andersen Consulting
	McKinsey & Co
Marketing	Inchcape plc
Media	Aegis Group plc
Merchant bank	Kleinwort Benson Group plc
Metal processing	Glynwed International plc
Mining	RTZ Corporation plc
Office equipment	Philips Dictation Systems
Oil	Royal Dutch/Shell Group of Companies
Paper	Bowater plc
Pharmaceuticals	Bayer AG
	Glaxo Holdings plc
	Johnson & Johnson
	Marion Merrell Dow Inc.
	Wellcome plc
Property	MEPC plc
Public relations	Burson-Marsteller
	Shandwick plc
Publishing	Reed Elsevier
Restaurants	McDonald's Restaurants Ltd
Retailing	The Boots Co plc
	JC Penney Co Inc
	John Menzies Group plc
	Kwik Save Group plc
	Marks & Spencer
	Safeway Stores plc

Other Kogan Page books by the same author:

101 Ways to Generate Great Ideas
101 Ways to Get Great Publicity
101 Ways to Get More Business
101 Ways to Succeed as an Independent Consultant
Winning Ways for Business in Europe

Other titles in the 101 Ways series:

101 Ways to Clean Up Your Act
101 Ways to Make More Profits
101 Ways to Start Your Own Business